Reading Comprehension

Stories of the Saints

Volume IV

By Elaine Woodfield

Illustrations by Kim Staggenborg

CATHOLIC HERITAGE CURRICULA

www.chcweb.com 1-800-490-7713

Dedication

In honor of the Divine Mercy
and for my daughter Jillian

Acknowledgments

We would like to thank the Sisters of the Blessed Sacrament
for the photos of St. Katharine Drexel;

Fr. Morgan Costelloe for providing the
painting of Ven. Matt Talbot and for his generous help;

the Canossian Daughters of Charity for the photos and
paintings of St. Josephine Bakhita.

ISBN: 978-0-9851642-7-0

Printed by Bookmasters
Ashland, Ohio
March 2019
Print code: 28242

CONTENTS

How to Use the Stories of the Saints

Introduction

What is a saint? A saint is a person who lived a heroic life of love and service of God and neighbor, and who is now happy with God in Heaven. The saints are our older brothers and sisters in God's family. They are very interested in our lives, and lovingly pray for us so that we may safely reach our Heavenly home. When we ask the saints to pray for us and help us, their gratefulness knows no bounds.

The saints are for our inspiration and imitation. Each saint story illustrates how that particular saint truly lived out, or embodied, the teachings of the gospel and of the catechism. It is true that the gospel and the catechism are books that must be learned well. But even more importantly, the gospel and the catechism must truly be lived. They are books that must be "written in our hearts." The saints teach us the way to do this like good older brothers and sisters should; likewise, they inspire us to greater love and service of God and neighbor.

Vocabulary, Terms to Know

A list of vocabulary words and terms have been prepared for each story. The reader should familiarize himself with the definitions before beginning each story. In this way, the reader will understand the story better. Looking the words up builds dictionary skills. There is no need to prepare a list of dictionary-type definitions. Instead, each reader should have a good working knowledge of the word list. For example, an acceptable definition for "segregate" is "to set apart or isolate a group of people."

There are many vocabulary words and terms having to do with Catholic life and teaching. Words are important tools for our understanding of God's plan of salvation.

Comprehension Questions

The comprehension questions should be completed after the story is read. The most thorough way to learn the story is to answer the questions using complete sentences. The sequence of the questions follows the sequence of the story. The answers need not be verbatim quotes from the story, but each answer should show an accurate understanding of the story.

Although an answer key is provided, the reader's answers need not be exact. As long as the answer conveys the proper meaning, it is correct. If a reader understands the question in a different way than intended by the author, and can prove his or her answer from the text, the answer is also considered correct.

Analyze This, Essay Questions

These lesson activities encourage the reader to go beneath the surface of the stories and try to understand the heart, faith and motivation of the saints. This helps the reader to connect the saints choices with his or her own choices in life.

Quotes

Memorizing quotations of the saints is a great way to train one's memory, and it's also a great way to keep in mind a prayer or a thought for holy living! The quotation becomes part of us, as if it were "written in our heart."

Geography and History, Research and Report

Researching the geography, history of the time and country of each saint gives the reader a closer look at the saint's life. What world-rocking events did the saint have to cope with? What cultural and historical influences was the saint affected by?

You, The Biographer

Each person in the list has influenced in some way the life of the saints in these stories. Many, though divided by several centuries and different cultures, made a profound impact on the saints' lives.

Putting Your Faith into Practice

The projects are provided as ways the reader can imitate the saints in living our Faith. Not all the projects are required, though they may be completed over a four-week period if desired. These projects can be a springboard for further serious study and appreciation of the Faith.

Special Usage

A family, classroom teacher, or a homeschooling parent of a reluctant reader may wish to modify these instructions to his or her particular situation. A family may wish to do the vocabulary and comprehension questions together orally, and then choose one additional section to do together. Or else, each family member may choose his/her own preferred section to complete. Or, a family may simply want to read the stories aloud in the evening.

A classroom teacher may obtain copies for each student, and have the story read orally by students in class. Then each student may do the vocabulary and comprehension questions on paper, and choose an additional section to complete. Another approach is for the teacher to read the story to his/her class, have the class do the vocabulary and comprehension questions orally, and then do one of the additional sections as a class.

A parent of a reluctant reader may have their reader learn the vocabulary orally and answer the comprehension questions orally as well. A homeschooling family with two or more readers may want to look up the definitions and question answers as a group project, assigning a portion to each child to do but requiring that all learn the definitions and answers.

In Conclusion

My hope is that you will become interested enough in these saints to read their full biographies. If each reader makes friends with at least one saint in these stories, I will consider them a wonderful success!

Elaine Woodfield

St. Katharine Drexel

To Know Christ Jesus

Philadelphia, Pennsylvania: 1885

It was to be a day of great contrasts and great destiny. East would meet West, rich would meet poor, need would meet fulfillment. To Kate Drexel, it seemed like an ordinary day. Little did she know, it would change her life.

As she sat upstairs in her Philadelphia mansion with her sisters, Kate had no way of knowing what a difference she would make in American history. She would help to change the face of America, and change the way Americans thought about themselves. She would do this by giving Christ Jesus to those who might otherwise not know Him. She would give hope to those who had none. Most of all, she would give herself.

Kate was searching for a way to do just that. She and her sisters were in an unusual situation. Their beloved father Francis had died suddenly that year; their mother had died two years before. Elizabeth, Katharine, and Louise Drexel were heiresses to a fortune of $14 million. This was an enormous sum of money in those days. Kate wished she had her parents back instead. The family had been a close-knit one, and the sisters were grief-stricken at losing their parents. Now Kate needed to plan her own future. She wanted to serve God with all her heart, and she was searching for her own vocation.

It all began with a knock at the large front door.

After answering it, the butler came upstairs.

"Two gentlemen, priests, to see the Misses Drexel," he announced.

Elizabeth, Kate, and Louise looked at one another. Visitors? They hadn't been expecting any. Louise broke the silence. "Kate, you go down," she suggested.

Nodding calmly, Kate arose and went downstairs. She was twenty-seven, a pretty young woman with a lively, kind personality that attracted many friends. She and her sisters had carried on the Drexel tradition of sharing their wealth with the poor. Many people, missionary priests included, made appeals to them for charitable donations. As she descended the stairs, Kate figured that her visitors arrived to make just such an appeal to her.

Little did she know, they would give her more than she could ever give them. By giving her a window onto another world, they would give her a whole new life.

Bishop Martin Marty and Fr. Joseph Stephen greeted her. They were missionary priests from the West. They came right to the point. The two missionaries requested funds to build and run Catholic schools for Indian children. These men had spent many years of tough hardship out West among the Indians and knew their needs well.

Kate was a true banker's daughter. She readily agreed to help, but she asked the two priests to give her details about the Indians and their plight. The priests agreed readily. As they spoke, Kate was transported in thought to a rugged land far from her comfortable home.

It all came down to the failure of President Grant's Peace Policy for the Indians, they said. This Peace Policy had seemed like a good idea at the time, but it had ended in disaster. The Indians were made poorer than ever, and most were without any hope of an education that would enable them to have a better life. How had the situation come to this?

White settlers, businessmen, and armies had moved in on the Indians' land; and they were not content to coexist peacefully with the Indians. Rather, they stole the best land from them. Each time this happened, the Indians would protest either by word or by going to war. Finally, both sides would compromise and sign a treaty. Then the whites would break the treaty and take what they wanted. In fact, there were few treaties between Indians and whites in which the whites kept their promises. In most cases, the Indians were forced to live on reservations, often on land they did not want.

This pattern repeated itself again and again with the many different Indian tribes throughout the country. The only people who seemed to care about the Indians were Protestant and Catholic missionaries. They built churches and schools to serve the Indians.

So President Grant came up with his Peace Policy. The United States government would pay a yearly fee to church schools as tuition for Indian children. This, of course, would help the church schools educate Indians. But there was a problem. Using railroads, rivers, and other landmarks as dividing lines, the government decided which Indian tribes would attend which schools. Many of the Indians were Christian, and now could not go to the church school of their choice. Catholic Indians were deprived of the Catholic education and sacraments they wanted. The Indians themselves objected to having these circumstances forced upon them.

Many Indian leaders unsuccessfully petitioned the United States government about this situation. To make matters worse, nearly all of the Protestant missions pulled out of Indian country one by one. Many tribes now had no school at all. The government itself then turned against the Policy, and by the 1880s, it was all but dead. The Indians were worse off than before.

Catholic missionaries were committed to staying with the Indians and helping them materially and spiritually. Bishop Marty and Fr. Stephen were two such missionaries. They had compassion on the Indians and wanted to bring even more of them to know Christ Jesus. They also wanted to educate them so that they could come out of poverty. Building Catholic schools was the perfect way to do both.

Kate listened intently, and she asked a lot of questions. As the priests finished their story, Kate remembered an experience she had as a child.

Kate at seven years old

She was sitting in a big, comfortable chair, reading a book. In it was a picture of Christopher Columbus as he stepped ashore in the New World. From behind trees, Indians were looking at Columbus with shyness and curiosity. As Kate looked at the Indians in the picture, she had a sudden realization: the reason Columbus came to the New World was to save the souls of the Indians!

The desire to help save the souls of these noble people was planted in little Kate's soul that day, and it grew with the years. Kate's happiest day was the day of her First Holy Communion at age eleven because she was united so closely to Christ Jesus. She wanted to give Jesus in the Blessed Sacrament to everyone. Likewise, she wanted to serve others for the love of God. Kate began to donate money to help the Indians. She realized that many people had made great sacrifices to bring the Faith to the Indians.

Kate knew that two such people sat before her now. As they described the dire poverty of the Indians, she resolved to do something for them. She decided to make service to the Indians her life's work.

Little did she know that in a few short years, she would decide to give the Indians not only her fortune but also her whole life. Kate would also extend this generous offering to people of color, namely, Americans of African descent. In serving these two neglected groups, Katharine Drexel would help to change the face of America and change the way Americans thought about themselves. Most important of all, her work would bring Christ Jesus to countless souls.

Who is Katharine Drexel?

Katharine Drexel was born in Philadelphia, Pennsylvania, on November 26, 1858. Her father, Francis, was a wealthy banker from the Drexel banking family. She had an older sister named Elizabeth. Her mother, Hanna, died only five weeks after Katharine was born. An aunt took care of the two little girls for two years. At that time, Francis Drexel married Emma Bouvier, and a few years later, their daughter Louise was born.

The Drexel family was a very close one. Francis was

Hanna Longstroth

6

a busy banker, but his family came first in his life. Emma loved and cared for all three girls as her own. In fact, her motherly love was so complete that Kate was thirteen before she realized that Emma was not her biological mother!

Francis Drexel

Emma was a well-educated woman, and she wanted to give the advantages of a good education to her daughters. Educated by tutors at home, the Drexel sisters learned a variety of subjects, including French, Latin, philosophy, and theology. Emma also made sure that the girls learned how to sew and cook, as well as run a large household. By their teens, the sisters knew how to manage a home, run a kitchen, manage gardens and stables, and purchase supplies.

The Drexel family's Catholic Faith was by far their most precious possession. One of Emma's first deeds after she married Francis was to set aside a room in their home and furnish it as a chapel. No matter how busy they were, the Drexels prayed together as a family each evening. Upon his return home from work, Francis Drexel devoted a half hour each day to private prayer; his family knew not to disturb him then.

Emma Bouvier Drexel

Emma believed in putting faith into action, and likewise she believed that wealthy people should help the poor. She ran her own charity agency three days per week. People in trouble or "down on their luck" came to the Drexel home to meet with Emma on those days and present their requests to her. She employed an investigator whose job was to make sure that the petitioner's need was real. Once convinced of this, she gave to the poor generously. Emma found jobs for people, befriended the sick, and supported the destitute. When she was older, Kate worked with Emma in her agency two days a week. The lessons Kate learned there would bear great fruit in her future.

The Drexels were part of an elite social group, the highest level of Philadelphia society. It was a world of the finest wines and cigars, expensive clothes, carriages, and mansions; plenty of parties, dances, balls, and concerts; and lots of servants to keep everything running smoothly. But the Drexels did not mix very much with this world; they did so only to be courteous.

In fact, in order to lead a quieter life, they moved to Torresdale, Pennsylvania, to a rural estate that they named St. Michael's. Kate loved it at Torresdale. She and her teenage sisters set up classes to teach catechism to several dozen children who lived on the estate, mainly sons and daughters of servants. Kate loved Christmastime when she gave these children presents, things both useful and fun, and watched smiles light up their faces.

When Kate was around twenty, two major things happened to her. First, she came to the end of her schooling in 1878. Her education had made her intelligent, cultured, and perceptive.

Kate as debutante

Yet she wrote in a letter:

> This will be a perpetual vacation for me, and yet strange to say, I do not feel particularly hilarious at the prospect. One looks forward so many years to finishing school, and when at last the time comes, a kind of sadness steals over one that is hard to analyze.

Kate was already considering her future, but to her it still looked "all vague and uncertain."

Second, Kate was "introduced into society" in 1879. This was also known as "coming out" or "making one's debut." A girl who had "been presented" at all the mandatory balls was considered to be an adult woman in high society. It was a time of new, expensive clothes and jewels, as well as lots of balls, receptions, and parties.

Kate gave this event barely a mention in one of her letters!

Even at a young age, Kate disliked being the center of attention. The wealth and glitter surrounding her did not impress her at all. She liked getting together with young people her own age—she had many friends—but she found herself less and less content with her life. It was God Whom she was seeking.

Kate kept notes of her spiritual resolutions and her progress (or lack of it) in them. What these notes lack in grammatical correctness, they make up for in zeal. One Lent, she resolved:

1. Not to eat between meals.
2. Not to take water between meals.
3. Dinner, everything but once.
4. No butter, no fruit.
5. To speak French.
6. To give money to the poor.

She made some rules for herself in 1876. Her notes say:

1. Never omit my morning prayers but to devote from 5 to 8 minutes in the morning to devotions in a prayer book.
2. During the day or if I prefer when clock strikes, offer all my actions to God.
3. Make meditation in Following of Christ or other book for about 10 or 15 minutes or perhaps less times.
4. Read a life of a saint or some good book such as "The Monks of the West" every three months. Novels of the day every once in a while.
5. Examine conscience thoroughly every day and see if the duties proposed have been fulfilled.

Kate kept track of her progress.

Jan	about the same
April	a little better
May	a little better with God's help
June	slight relaxation from the last
July, Aug, Sept	I think relaxed
Now	relaxed

She didn't let failure deter her; rather, she kept trying. Every day, she prayed that she might know her vocation in life.

An answer to this prayer came in an unexpected way.

In late 1879, Emma Drexel felt herself getting more and more tired and weak. Pain came and went. A doctor told her that she needed a minor operation. Since she did not want to worry her family, Emma made arrangements for her doctor to operate on her at home!

Telling her family at Torresdale that she needed to plan some renovations for their Philadelphia home, she went there and had her operation. Soon it was clear that she had cancer, and there was nothing anyone could do.

Kate was stunned. It had never occurred to her that anyone in her family circle could die so young. She stayed with Emma to nurse her in her sickness, which lasted for three years. In those days, it was thought that a change of scenery or climate could help cure a sick person. Emma traveled to Colorado and to rural New York State, but nothing helped.

During the last year of her life, Emma suffered greatly from pain. Kate was ever at her side. During these long months, Kate thought deeply about life and her own existence. She knew that Emma was a good woman. Yet she suffered agony from cancer. Did she deserve this? Of course not. Then why did Emma suffer?

Kate soon realized that it was through original sin that suffering and death entered the world. Through Emma's suffering, Kate could see the effects of original sin in all their horror. Kate was reminded of Jesus suffering on the cross to redeem us. The only thing that could console Jesus in His suffering was the saving of souls; indeed, this was the purpose of His life and His death. Kate came to realize that bringing souls to Jesus was the most important work anyone could do.

Kate also learned a lesson about faith at her mother's bedside. Emma embraced the will of God in her suffering and accepted what was happening to her. Her faith only grew. She offered her pain so that her husband Francis would not suffer when he died. Kate remembered her mother's surrender to God all her life.

During the long hours at Emma's bedside, Kate's thoughts turned to her own life. All Emma's wealth, beauty, and intelligence did not help her in her last journey. Only her faith mattered. Kate had the same thought over and over: she should give her life completely to God as a nun.

After suffering for three years, Emma died in February of 1883. She was mourned by the hundreds of poor people she had helped, as well as many others whom she had impressed. The Drexels drew even closer together in their grief. Francis took his daughters on a train trip to the Far West; he had business to conduct there, but the real purpose was to give everyone a change of scenery to help heal their loss. At this time, Kate wrote to Bishop O'Connor about her desire for the religious life. He advised her to "think, pray, wait."

This she did while doing her charitable work and helping to run the Drexel home. She did not have long to wait for another tragedy to come. Francis caught what looked like a routine cold. He developed pleurisy, but it did not seem to be a bad case. Francis died suddenly and quietly in February 1885. The Drexel sisters were nearly overwhelmed with grief; they drew closer still.

They had ample means for their own support and that of their charities because their father's will was an unusual one. He had a fortune of $15 million, an enormous amount of money in those days. Francis had arranged that $1 million be given right away to a large number of his favorite Philadelphia charities: hospitals, schools, orphanages, and the like. The remaining $14 million would be held in trust for his daughters, who were able to live off the income generated by the interest from this fortune but could not touch the original $14 million in principal.

Francis did not want any young men to marry his daughters for their money, so one clause of his will said that only his daughters could deal with the Drexel fortune. The $14 million, upon the death of the last Drexel daughter, would go to their children. If there were none, the money would be distributed among the various charities that had benefited from his generosity when he died. So Elizabeth, Kate, and Louisa's income was about $1000 a day.

Kate would rather have had her father back. Grief for her parents took its toll on her. Her health was in a weak state when Bishop Marty and Fr. Stephen visited her and changed her life.

*   *   *   *

Kate felt the peace of having true purpose. She set to work to help the Indians in a practical fashion; she researched, wrote letters, and asked questions. Yet her illness worsened. She developed jaundice, so in the summer of 1886, she and her sisters set sail for Europe, hoping the trip would help cure Kate.

The trip had a second purpose. All three sisters were in the midst of planning, building, and staffing schools for the poor. Louise founded the St. Emma Industrial School for young black men. Elizabeth was concerned that young people from orphanages had no work training, so she founded the St. Francis Industrial School for orphans of any race. And Kate, of course, worked on founding missions for Indians and supporting schools for black children.

Realizing that there was a lot that they did not know, they planned visits to charitable schools in Europe to see how they were run. There were few, if any, such schools in America at the time.

Kate stayed at the Schwalbach Spa for five weeks and emerged cured of her illness. She then rode in luxurious trains, stayed at fine hotels, and ate gourmet meals while traveling throughout Europe. She could well appreciate the beauty of the painting, sculpture, architecture, and music that was so abundant in Europe. Yet Kate's attention remained on the Indian missions and on how she could best help them.

She visited schools in Europe, taking many notes on how they were run. Fr. Stephen flooded her with letters about the many missions she was helping. The shortage of mission priests was a pressing problem. He asked Kate if she could make this need known in Europe, in the hope of recruiting priests there; Kate agreed

While touring the splendors of Venice, she came upon a lovely statue of Our Lady in a church. Kneeling, she said a prayer. All of a sudden, she heard a woman's voice speak clearly:

"Freely have you received; freely give."

Was this Our Lady's voice? Or was it Kate's imagination? She wondered, but yet, she knew that the words were true. She had received much: the love of a close family, an excellent education, a strong and dynamic Catholic Faith, the spur of good example, and great wealth. All she wanted was to give of herself to God. But how?

Another answer came to her in an unusual way.

The Drexel sisters were granted an audience with Pope Leo XIII. Kate herself was able to have a conversation with him; she told him of her work with Fr. Stephen and his need of missionary priests to serve the Indians. The Pope himself had a missionary spirit, and he easily understood the complex needs of the missions.

Smiling gently at her, Pope Leo leaned toward her.

"Why not, my child, yourself become a missionary?" he asked.

Kate drew back. Herself? She was seeking priests. Had the Holy Father misunderstood? She knew that he had not.

Somehow the audience ended. In a daze, Kate found herself outside. She began weeping uncontrollably. To become a missionary was not in her plans. She wanted to give away her fortune all at once to the missions. She then wanted to become a contemplative nun so that she could receive and adore Jesus in the Eucharist every day. In this way, she could help the missions by her prayers.

Kate and her sisters sailed for home, arriving in April 1887. A seed was planted in Kate's mind by her meeting with the Pope; it only needed time to grow.

In September of 1887, the Drexel sisters left for a trip to the West at Fr. Stephen's request. He urged them "to see for themselves" the missionary needs of the West. Travel past the railroads was rough. Kate rode in a carriage with Bishop O'Connor and Fr. Stephen while her irrepressible sisters rode their saddle horses across the Great Plains. They passed hills and ravines, rivers and rocks, ever riding to the end of a vast horizon.

They visited St. Francis Mission in Rosebud Agency and the Holy Rosary Mission in Pine Bluff Agency. Here they met many Sioux Indians, the most important of whom was Chief Red Cloud. As Fr. Stephen told him of the Drexels' plan to build a school for Indian children and to expand the mission, he approved. The Drexel sisters impressed him with their interest and sincerity. They paid him the highest honor by visiting him in his home and presenting him and his wife with thoughtful gifts. Kate was appalled at the poverty in which many of the Indians lived. This made her even more determined to help them.

Western visit

After visiting other missions in North and South Dakota, they returned home. Kate's mind was full of plans for erecting buildings, purchasing land, drilling for water, supplying schools, and the like. She hired builders and sent checks; she contacted religious orders and arranged to staff or expand her missions. She made arrangements for government tuition for each Indian student to be sent to the appropriate mission.

Kate worked quietly, but her results were spectacular. In five years' time, she had built and staffed schools and missions throughout the West. These missions served the Pueblo Indians of New Mexico; the Osages, Cherokees, and Comanches of the Indian Territory and Oklahoma; the Blackfeet and Crows of Montana; the Chippewas in Wisconsin; the Sioux in the Dakotas; the Cheyennes and Arapahos in Wyoming; the Coeur d'Alene and Nez Perce in Idaho; the Puyallups of Washington State; and the Mission Indians of California.

Kate continued to struggle with her vocation question. She was torn: she wanted to be a contemplative sister, but she also wanted to continue helping the Indians and people of color because no one else was. As a student of history, Kate knew that the Indians had suffered great injustice during the Western Expansion. Likewise, slaves who had been made free by the Civil War began their lives of freedom with little or nothing. In the South especially, they were segregated from whites and denied the basics of decent employment, housing, and schooling. These Americans of African descent made great strides in spite of nearly insurmountable odds, but there was a long way to go. Kate seized nearly every opportunity to help these neglected groups. She wanted to give her money to a bureau of a religious order that would help Indians and people of color, but no one was as committed to helping these groups as she was.

Kate also wanted to make reparation for the great injustices suffered by these people. Reparation is best made in person. Kate was coming to the conclusion that she needed to found her own religious order.

She shrank from the idea. She knew she was not a born leader, and she did not feel worthy. Didn't only saints found religious orders? Kate was not even a nun herself, and she knew very little about day-to-day living in a religious order, let alone how to start one. Yet she knew that if she did not act, perhaps no one would. She had the opportunity to lead a group of sisters who would give their very lives in service to Indians and people of color. She had the opportunity to answer a call from God.

Bishop O'Connor put it into perspective for her in one of his letters:

> It's all right, Kate. It's like an invitation to a wedding; you don't have to take it if you don't want to. But if you do take it, it may mean that thousands of souls will know God who otherwise could never have known Him.

That decided her. Kate came up with a plan. She entered the convent of the Mercy Sisters in Pittsburgh in May of 1889 to learn the religious life.

This banker's daughter edified all the Mercy Sisters by her humility and willingness to learn. Kate obeyed all orders promptly, and she did so with cheerfulness. She wanted to practice holy poverty like her hero St. Francis of Assisi, so she let nothing go to waste. She cut unused strips of paper from letters to use for her notes, and she mended her dinner napkin rather than throw it away. Kate even entertained the other sisters at recreation by demonstrating the Indian dances she had learned out West.

Happy and peaceful in the novitiate, Kate learned the basics of nursing and teaching. As she worked at the school for black children run by the Sisters, it was clear that Kate was not a very good teacher. Sensing that she was new at teaching, one of her students brought a whistle to class. Kate asked him to give it to her, and instead of doing this, he blew it loudly. This was the signal for complete chaos: children raced in a circle around the room, a lively fistfight broke out, and someone kindled a roaring fire in the fireplace! Kate had seen another sister restore order to her class by sitting at her desk and glaring at her students over her eyeglasses. So she did this.

"Children! No more lessons until there is perfect silence in this room," she said to them. All of a sudden, the entire class burst out singing a hymn at the top of their lungs! This brought the sister in the next classroom over, and she restored discipline in short order.

Kate herself was quite amused at her own ineptitude, admitting that she was much better at nursing.

While continuing her missionary correspondence during her novitiate, Kate also made plans for her own religious order. She attracted a lot of attention in November of 1889 on the occasion of taking her vows as a religious sister. Kate entered the chapel dressed in a white wedding gown trimmed with orange blossoms. She wore diamond rings and a diamond necklace, and eight little girls in white satin dresses attended her. No bride looked more beautiful! After making her vows, Kate left the chapel, and appeared shortly afterward, dressed as a nun. Kate's happiness was complete: she was a Bride of Christ.

Many newspapers across the country wrote stories about this event. After all, an heiress to a fortune giving up her wealth to live a life of poverty to save souls was certainly newsworthy! These newspaper stories cropped up from time to time throughout Sr. Katharine's life. As one reporter from Boston put it a half-century later:

> If we would understand this remarkable figure, we must try to remember two facts: There have been at all times men and women who have given their lives to saving souls of their fellows. Every human being has a soul worth saving.

Kate shunned publicity, but it had one benefit: it attracted other young women to join her.

These quiet years of preparation had their share of drama. The Wounded Knee Massacre took place near her Holy Rosary Mission. Chief Red Cloud, remembering the dedication of Kate and her sisters to the Indians, intervened to save the Mission and its sisters. Sr. Katharine's prayers were with the Indians and her mission.

Another grief came when Bishop O'Connor died in 1890. Bishop Ryan, a family friend, took his place and remained a good friend and advisor to her and her new order. Sr. Katharine's sister Elizabeth got married and soon was expecting a baby. The family was delighted. But in September of 1890, Elizabeth and her baby died in childbirth. Sr. Katharine offered up her grief to God.

First Profession of Sr. Mary Katharine

Not even these tragedies could deter Katharine Drexel. She trained her new sisters, made plans with her missionaries, and started her new religious order. It was called the Sisters of the Blessed Sacrament for Indians and Colored People. Kate was now Mother Katharine. She bought a sixty-acre parcel of land in a place called Cornwells Heights, Pennsylvania, for her order's Motherhouse. As it was being built, Mother Katharine and her sisters used St. Michael's at Torresdale as their first Motherhouse. Her sisters were eager to go out West as soon as possible, for it seemed that they were greatly needed at St. Stephen's Mission in Wyoming.

Mother Katharine had arranged for the building of a new school and convent at this mission. But nothing went right. The workmen squabbled with the Jesuit priests in charge of the mission. The buildings were finally built, but the foundation was laid too shallow, and the walls were on the verge of collapsing. Finally, all was put right, and the Sisters of Charity from Kansas came to staff the school. But the sisters were needed by their order due to a shortage of sisters, so they returned home. Some Protestant women were hired as teachers, but for some reason, this did not work out either. The school now stood empty.

Mother Katharine and Sr. Patrick traveled to the West by train, stagecoach, and ferryboat to untangle the mess. By asking questions, taking notes, and making suggestions, she put things right. Traveling back East, she purchased supplies for the school and convent and put them in crates for shipments. All was ready.

But she was in for a surprise. Bishop Ryan would not give her permission to send her sisters to St. Stephen's! He had good reason for this decision. Most of the sisters were very new to religious life, and to go out West at this early state might destroy the new order. Mother Katharine was disappointed, but she accepted this decision. Years later, she said, "Oh, how audacious I was in those days. Almighty God was certainly good to save us from such a mistake. I see now what a wild scheme it was. It could have been the ruination of our little Congregation." In due time, St. Stephen's was filled with Arapaho and Shoshone Indian children.

The order of the Sisters of the Blessed Sacrament grew and grew. Mother Katharine started the mission of St. Catharine in New Mexico for the Pueblo Indians. This mission experienced the same kinds of problems as St. Stephen's had. But it was a great day when nine Sisters of the Blessed Sacrament arrived at St. Catharine's to begin teaching the Pueblo children.

Success was not always easy. Fr. Stephen told her of the desire of the Navajo Indians "to get Catholic missionaries" in 1895. So she purchased a desert oasis in Arizona the next year. She learned all she could about the Navajos, and searched for priests to serve them. Finally she found Franciscan priests from Cincinnati whose zeal and enthusiasm matched her own; they agreed gladly to serve the Navajos. Mother Katharine paid all their expenses, and arranged for the old trading post on the oasis to be renovated. The Franciscans arrived at the mission in 1898.

Mother Mary Katharine with the Navajos in Arizona

The priests knew no Navajo and the Navajos knew no English, so the priests began to learn this beautiful and difficult language. One of them did this by holding up a mail-order catalog, pointing to a picture, and asking the Navajo word for that object! Eventually, these Franciscans compiled the first dictionary of the Navajo language. The Navajos respected the Franciscans for their earnest efforts to learn their language and accepted them completely.

In 1900 Mother Katharine visited the mission, now called St. Michael's, and made plans for a school. Once back East, she wrote letters to the Franciscans back at the mission. No detail was too small for her to notice: locating water for a well, getting rid of rats and mice, the transporting of supplies by freight, and even the rising of a nearby creek all attracted and received her attention. But building went slowly; in 1901 and again in 1902 she visited and had to put things right.

In 1902, St. Michael's School opened with twelve Sisters of the Blessed Sacrament staffing it. But there were few students! The Navajos were not used to the idea of a school for their children, preferring to keep them at home. Fr. Anselm rode on horseback for months to visit and convince the Navajo parents. By December, forty-seven children came—with their parents! The sisters conducted classes in English for about two weeks while the Navajo children and parents watched them silently. Finally, the parents began to trust the sisters and willingly left their children with them. St. Michael's School has enjoyed steady growth ever since!

Mother Katharine traveled throughout the West and South, visiting and founding missions and schools. Every so often, a newspaper would do a story on her, which would bring a flood of mission appeals in its wake. But more and more women joined her. They agreed with her theory that education lifts people out of poverty. So as the appeals grew, so did the number of sisters to fill them.

In the South, Mother Katharine was up against stiff opposition to her plans. After the Civil War, blacks and whites were segregated from one another in nearly all aspects of public life. The Plessy vs. Ferguson decision of the Supreme Court made separate but equal facilities legal. They were separate indeed but certainly not equal. Mother Katharine sought to make things more equal. It was her dream that someday segregation would be illegal, so she prepared for that future by founding and funding schools for black children in the South and in the big cities of the North, such as Chicago and Harlem.

She had her work cut out for her. For example, in Montgomery, Alabama, there were no schools for black children at all. When she did set up a new school, she often had to deal with bomb threats, legal action, and signed petitions to try to make her and her sisters leave. But she went forward, one school at a time, and in time, there were dozens of them throughout the South.

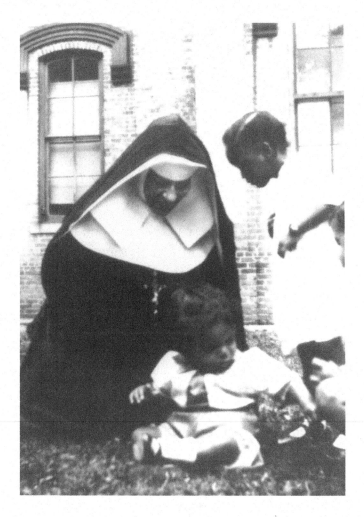

Mother Katharine's most impressive achievement took place in New Orleans. The state of the Louisiana school system was a deplorable one at the turn of the twentieth century. A white child attended school from anywhere between four to eight months; a black child could count on no more than three to six months. The Sisters of the Holy Family did a wonderful job building and running schools for black children, which gave them an excellent education, and Mother Katharine gladly gave them her support. But there were very few colleges for black students who wished to continue their education.

Planning to change this, Mother Katharine bought the land and buildings of the former site of Southern University for $18,000 in 1915. Its white neighbors had petitioned the state that this university for black students be moved to Baton Rouge, so its buildings had stood empty until Mother Katharine bought them.

What a furor she caused! Petition followed petition for many years, but nothing could deter her. Years before, she had written some resolutions for herself:

> You have no time to occupy your thoughts with that complacency of consideration of what others would think. Your business is simply, "What will my Father in Heaven think."

She named the place Xavier Preparatory School, brought in her sisters, and hired more teachers. Soon grades seven through twelve were full. Before long, Xavier also became a college, or "normal school," and was graduating qualified teachers. Filling a real need, Xavier grew so much that Mother Katharine had to buy bigger grounds and build bigger buildings. Other colleges were added. Xavier University grew to be an impressive place!

Mother Katharine continued to travel throughout the South to inspect her schools and plan new ones. She and her friend Mother Xavier agreed to travel by boat in the bayou country of Louisiana with Fr. Jean Marie Girault. This extraordinary priest came from a wealthy and noble French family, but he had dedicated his life to serve the Louisiana poor of the bayou country.

And they were indeed poor. Bayou children were lucky if they attended school for two months a year. Most black children of the bayou had one month a year of schooling, or none at all. Mother Katharine was appalled at what she saw. The area school was often a tumbledown shack or hut, and supplies were scarce. But she loved the bayou people who so cheerfully made the best of things. When Fr. Girault arrived at a settlement, he fired his gun into the air. This brought his parishioners quickly to the riverbank to give Father and his guests an enthusiastic welcome! The parishioners agreed with Mother Katharine's idea that education lifts people out of poverty and supported her plans.

And they were big plans indeed. Mother Katharine had twenty-four schools for black children built in the bayou country—all at the same time. She hired Xavier University graduates as teachers, and she paid their salaries for many years. These schools grew and grew, and soon parish churches were built near many of them!

Mother Katharine was happy to see how her schools strengthened the Catholic Faith. No student was ever forced to join the Church, or even made to attend Mass; following Catholic principles, Mother believed in true freedom of conscience for everyone. But her zeal attracted many people to the Catholic Faith, and it likewise strengthened the faith of Catholics. Believing in the Mystical Body of Christ, Mother Katharine knew that when one person is helped, then everyone shares in the blessing. She rejoiced with every graduate of her schools who now was better prepared for success.

The year 1935 was an unusually busy one for Mother Katharine. Now seventy-seven years old, she traveled to visit her missions in the South, in the rugged country of Washington State, and in the West. In South Dakota, she learned that some young Indian women wanted to start a new religious order for Indian women. As nuns, they would serve their fellow Indians. Mother Katharine gladly provided them with the help and advice they needed to get started, even "lending" them some of her sisters. She remembered how kind the Mercy Sisters had been to her, and she was grateful for the opportunity to share this kindness with others.

When she made a stop in Chicago to arrange for medical care for one of her sisters, Mother Katharine had a heart attack, a very bad one. She returned to the Motherhouse but had another serious heart attack the next year. In 1937, she was relieved of nearly all of her responsibilities. Other capable hands—sisters she had trained herself—ran her order and her missions.

In a way, this was a dream come true for Mother Katharine. She was free to pray all day, just as she had wished in the days of her vocation search. And pray she did. Her room had a balcony called the tribune, which looked onto the chapel. Mother Katharine spent most of her waking hours in her wheelchair, adoring Jesus in the Blessed Sacrament, praying for everyone, especially the children in her missions. During World War II, she prayed constantly for those in the bombed cities, the refugees and the soldiers, friends and foes alike; she left no one out.

As she kept in touch with the sisters at her missions by letter, Mother Katherine also wrote notes to herself during these years:

> Prayer can reach where the pen fails to go.
>
> Love does not consist of great sweetness of devotion, but in a most fervent determination to strive to please God in all things.
>
> Our Lord likes courage. Get it from Him. You won't find it in yourself.
>
> I have discovered how to pray in an extremely efficacious manner. The Heart of Jesus is also my heart since I am a member of His body and with this Heart I will pray to God, my Father, and my prayer will always be heard.
>
> The head of every person is Christ. He is the Head, we are the limbs. Is the Head to be crowned with thorns and the limbs to abound in comfort . . .?
>
> Time passes away, but not the eternal recompense. Pain is dealt out drop by drop, but if I properly endure it—or am sorry for my slips, the eternal recompense is a torrent of joy and peace.
>
> As bread is changed into Jesus Christ, so must I be changed into Jesus Christ so that He will live in me alone.
>
> My sweetest joy is to be in the presence of Jesus in the Holy Sacrament. I beg that when obliged to withdraw in body, I may leave my heart before the Holy Sacrament.
>
> Yes, my Lord, and my God Jesus, to You I commend my spirit, my soul with all its faculties, my body with its senses, my heart with its affections, all that I have, all that I am, that You may dispose of me absolutely in everything according to Your will. . . . O Jesus, I love you and Your Mother and abandon myself to Your love for time and eternity.

Ever humble, Mother Katharine looked upon her life as totally wasted:

> Blessed indeed am I who have seen and heard what I have from childhood, as a member of Holy Mother the Church, partaking of her sacraments. It is deplorable that I cannot bring forth one hundred fold; it is too late now to reach this but I can strive for a penitential life and not let one small opportunity pass.

The Fiftieth Jubilee of the Sisters of the Blessed Sacrament came in 1941, amid celebrations of every kind. Mother Katharine rejoiced with everyone for all the good done by her sisters. In 1943, her sister Louise died unexpectedly; the two of them had been very close, especially in their old age.

Growing weaker, Mother Katharine needed more and more care. One day, a sister came into her room.

"Do you see them?" asked Mother Katharine, looking up at a corner of her ceiling.

"See what?" asked the sister, who saw nothing unusual.

"The children," she answered.

The next morning, she said to the same sister, "Oh, all the children were there, all going past, so many of them. And the Pope was there too in all his regalia, and so many children. They were all there."

Was Mother Katharine seeing all the souls that her order had brought to Christ Jesus?

On March 3, 1955, Mother Katharine Drexel died peacefully. Crowds of people filed past her casket, many of them people she had helped, so many that the police had to direct traffic. Two hundred and fifty priests and countless others were at her funeral Mass, and two Indians, two blacks, and two whites were her pallbearers.

At the time of her death, the Sisters of the Blessed Sacrament ran forty-nine elementary schools, twelve high schools, one university, three social service houses, and one house of studies. Ten years after her death, there were over six hundred Sisters of the Blessed Sacrament. Mother Katharine Drexel had contributed to dozens, perhaps hundreds, of already-existing missions across the country and throughout the world.

The equality of all people is a concept we take for granted today, but it was not always so in our country. Many assumed that those who looked "different" should "keep to their place." Mother Katharine challenged this assumption by giving her life in service to Indians and people of color. After all, hadn't Jesus died for all? Because He loved them, she loved them:

> Love! love! Let us give ourselves to real pure love. Devotion to the Sacred Heart is a devotion which alone can banish the coldness of our time. The renewal which I seek and which we all seek is a work of love and can be accomplished by love alone.

Pope John Paul II canonized St. Katharine Drexel on October 1, 2000.

Lesson Activities
St. Katharine Drexel

Vocabulary

Define the following.

close-knit	realization	contemplative	vocation
missionary	desire	determined	bayou
coexist	resolve	segregate	conscience
compromise	elite	reparation	refugee
petition	meditation	deter	penitential

Terms to Know

Discover the meaning of each of the following.

Blessed Sacrament

Original Sin

Mystical Body of Christ

Western Expansion

Civil War

Comprehension Questions

Answer the following, using complete sentences.

1. What were the names of the two priests who knocked at Kate Drexel's door?

2. Who were they, and what did they want from Kate?

3. What effect did President Grant's Peace Policy have on the Indians?

4. How would you describe the Drexel family?

5. What two major things happened to Kate when she was about twenty?

6. Kate made spiritual resolutions and rules for herself. Was she always successful in keeping them?

7. What did Kate learn at Emma's bedside?

8. What question did Pope Leo XIII ask Kate?

9. Kate finally decided to found a new order of nuns to serve Indians and people of color. What did she do next?

10. At the same time, she was building and staffing missions throughout the West. List the states in which she had her first group of missions.

11. When Mother Katharine bought the land and buildings of Southern University in New Orleans, she caused a furor, but nothing could deter her. What resolution had she written years before?

12. What is this school called?

13. Mother Katharine toured the bayou country of Louisiana, and she was appalled at the poor condition of the schools. How long did black children of the bayou go to school each year?

14. What did Mother Katharine do to solve this problem?

15. Mother Katharine was relieved of her responsibilities in 1937 due to her poor health. Why was this a dream come true for her?

16. For whom did she pray?

Analyze This

Using as many details as you can, explain each question in paragraph form.

1. For what was Kate Drexel searching?

2. Why didn't President Grant's Peace Policy work?

3. Describe the Drexel family.

4. Why did Kate decide to serve Indians and people of color?

5. What did Kate do with her fortune?

6. How did publicity help the Sisters of the Blessed Sacrament?

7. How did Kate's schools benefit Indians and people of color?

8. How did Kate value a life of action and a life of prayer?

Essay Questions

Answer one or more of the following in essay form.

1. How did Kate Drexel's family life influence her as an adult?

2. How did the Drexel family live "in the world," yet remain "not of the world"?

3. In what way did Kate's lists of rules and resolutions help her throughout her life?

4. How did Emma's last illness change Kate's life?

5. How did Kate put into practice this quote: "Freely have you received; freely give"?

6. How did Kate's meeting with Pope Leo XIII influence her life?

7. Why is reparation best made in person?

8. In what ways was Kate ahead of her time?

9. What Gospel values did Kate's life exemplify?

Quotes

Complete one or more of the following.

1. Choose one or more quotes from St. Katharine Drexel, memorize it/them, and recite it/them.

2. Choose a quote from St. Katharine Drexel and explain it in essay form. You may wish to give a speech based on your composition.

Geography and History

Complete one or more of the following.

1. Using the place names in the story, draw and label a map of places in the life of St. Katharine Drexel.

2. Choose one or more Indian tribe from those mentioned in the story. Research all you can about the tribe: its history, customs, locations, and way of life. Write a report or make a display of examples of your findings. If possible, create an example of a craft made by the tribe. Or, make a replica of an artifact that was used by the tribe.

3. Do some research and write a brief report or speech on Christopher Columbus and the reasons for his voyages.

4. How did the policy of the United States government toward the Indians change over time? Research to answer this question, and relate your findings in written or oral form.

5. Research a brief historical sketch about the Civil War and its effect on persons of color in the South and in the North.

6. Draw a map of the United States, diagramming and labeling the ancestral territories of all the Indian tribes.

7. Pick one of St. Katharine Drexel's missions or schools. Research and diagram its buildings, layout, and growth over time.

8. Research and report on the Wounded Knee Massacre and its effect on the Indians and the government policy toward them.

Research and Report

Choose one or more of the following topics, and research and write a report about it. Be sure to include related maps, diagrams, time lines, and illustrations.

1. The United States government's policies toward Indians

2. The Western Expansion and its effect on American history

3. The life of a slave in the South

4. Segregation of black people and the victories of the Civil Rights Movement

5. Catholic missionaries and the West

6. Xavier University

7. The history of Catholic schools in America

8. The history of the city of Philadelphia

9. The Sisters of the Blessed Sacrament for Indians and Colored People—yesterday and today.

You, The Biographer

Research and write a biography of one or more of the persons listed below. Be sure to use at least two sources for your biography. You may wish to present it as a speech.

1. St. Francis of Assisi

2. Pope Leo XIII

3. Chief Red Cloud

4. President Ulysses S. Grant

5. Bishop Martin Marty

6. Fr. (Msgr.) Joseph Stephen

7. Christopher Columbus

8. Henriette Delille, the remarkable founder of the Sisters of the Holy Family in New Orleans

Putting Your Faith into Practice

Choose one or more of the following.

1. Jesus in the Blessed Sacrament was the center of St. Katharine Drexel's life. To give Christ in the Blessed Sacrament to others was the reason for all her missionary activities. What place did Jesus in the Blessed Sacrament have in the lives of the saints? Read several accounts of the lives of the saints, skimming them until you find information on the importance of Jesus in the Eucharist in their lives. Take some notes on each saint you research. Put your findings together in an essay, speech, reflection, poem, or story.

2. St. Katharine Drexel spent the last twenty years of her life in prayer before the Blessed Sacrament. Pay a visit to Jesus in the Blessed Sacrament once a week, and speak to Him from the heart through prayer. What difference does this make in your life?

3. Research and support a mission to Indians or people of color. You may wish to earn some money and send it to the mission. Try to contribute regularly, and keep in touch with your mission.

4. St. Katharine Drexel believed in passing on the Faith to others. As a teenager, she taught catechism to children. Become involved in catechetical instruction in some way. You may wish to become involved in your parish catechetical program, help a younger child in sacrament preparation, or teach religion to a younger sibling or friend.

5. We stand on the shoulders of others. Research and discover what role missionaries played in your local area, county, or state, or even your parish, in the past.

6. Imagine what your life would be like as an Indian or a person of color during the lifetime of St. Katharine Drexel, and write a creative story or play of your life from this point of view.

7. Imagine how it would be if you inherited a fortune. Do you think you would be a good steward of this money? Detail how you would spend your fortune.

To learn more about the life of St. Katharine Drexel visit: www.katharinedrexel.org

Venerable Matt Talbot

A Life Poured Out

Dublin, Ireland: One Saturday Morning, 1884

Matt Talbot and his brother Phil stood outside on a street corner, near one of their favorite bars. They had no money, and they both wanted a drink very much. The lack of money was no problem, as they saw it, because they had treated, or "stood rounds," for their friends many times when their friends had been short of cash. Being short of cash was a common occurrence in Dublin, where the average workman earned a low wage.

The previous week had been an unusual one for Matt. He skipped work for a whole week, which also was unusual for him because he was a diligent and hard worker. He put his time to "good use" at his favorite bars, or pubs, pursuing the only real interest he had. Drinking all week long, he had not drawn a sober breath until now, Saturday morning.

It was cold and damp, as Dublin mornings usually were, but thoughts of the warmth of drink and the conviviality of his drinking buddies helped to warm Matt as he waited. He remembered the clink of the glasses; the sounds of beer, wine, and whiskey being poured out; the sounds of laughter, arguments, and singing.

These were what Matt loved best in life. In a pub, a man could forget his desperate poverty and the grinding toil of his life. He could forget that a foreign power occupied Ireland

30

and made itself wealthy on the backs of the poor and hopeless. He could forget that home was poor and overcrowded and that dinner might be only bread and vegetables. A man could forget a lot in a Dublin pub, surrounded by his friends, glowing with the warmth of drink.

Matt spotted his first friend of the morning and greeted him warmly.

"Good mornin', Matt," answered the friend warily, as he walked on.

Matt was puzzled. No Irishman worth his salt wanted to drink alone. Matt expected his friend to ask him to join him. Perhaps the man was in the same dire straits as he was. Shrugging to himself, Matt continued to wait on the same corner so that he could greet his friends as they approached the pub from several different streets.

Another friend came into view. To Matt's surprise, the man crossed the street to avoid speaking to him! Another friend came, and another; after walking past the Talbot brothers, they hurried into the pub. Although some men greeted Matt and his brother, others crossed the street to avoid speaking to them, while still others pretended that they did not even see them. In all of them, there seemed to be wariness, a hesitation to be too friendly.

Matt Talbot was astounded.

What went through his mind as he watched his friends avoid him? No one knows. Matt was a friendly, well-liked man, but he always kept his personal thoughts to himself. Did he remember all the good times he'd had with all of these drinking buddies, or did he wonder what had changed? Something deep inside Matt Talbot changed.

"Let's go," he said to his brother. Phil objected.

"It's too early! Dinner won't be ready! Let's keep on waiting. Some of my friends are bound to turn up."

Matt shook his head, throbbing as it was from his hangover.

"I'm cut to the heart," he said simply. "You can stay. I'm going home."

Right there on the misty streets of Dublin, Matt Talbot had made a decision that would change his life. His resolve grew stronger as he walked home. When he arrived there, his mother looked at him with astonishment.

"You are home early, Matt," she exclaimed, "and you are sober." Matt had never come home early if there had been drinking to do, and he had not really been sober for the past sixteen years.

"Yes, mother, I am," he replied calmly. He stayed for the midday meal and remained at home afterward, which was unusual for him. He seemed thoughtful. Mrs. Talbot knew her son well; he would talk when he was ready. Finally he spoke. "I am going to take the pledge," Matt said to his mother.

"Go, in God's name," she said with a smile, "but don't take it unless you are going to keep it."

"I'll go, in God's name," he said.

"God give you strength to keep it," she said to him as he left. Full of unexpected joy, she multiplied her prayers for her son.

Anyone watching Matt Talbot walk down the streets of Dublin would see a short man who was thin and wiry, slightly balding, dressed in the clothes of a workingman, muffler wrapped around his neck against the wind. He looked ordinary, but this twenty-eight-year-old man was going to do something quite out of the ordinary. He was going to promise to stop drinking—he was going to "take the pledge."

Before Matt was born, the "pledge" originated with an active alcohol abstinence movement in Ireland, led by a dedicated priest. Thousands took the pledge and promised to give up drinking; but when the priest died, the movement lost its impetus. Still, the many successes of this movement were well known. The only way for an alcoholic to conquer the hold alcohol has on him or her is to promise never to drink again.

Ever.

Matt arrived at the chapel of Holy Cross College, which contained a relic of the True Cross, and sought out a priest. He spoke with the priest and told him what he wanted to do. The priest recommended that Matt go to Confession, attend Mass on Sunday, and receive Holy Communion. This seemed sensible to Matt. He went to Confession and then pledged to abstain from alcohol for three months. He was afraid to pledge more, he said later, but he put his trust in God for help. Waking up early the next morning, he went to Mass at 5 A.M., and he made sure that he was one of the first to receive Holy Communion. Matt seemed to know that the only way he would succeed was to rely on the sacraments to help him.

And rely on the sacraments he did. On Monday morning, Matt went again to Mass at 5 A.M. He made sure that he was the first one in line for Holy Communion because he wanted to be sure he was not late for work at 6 A.M., but he needn't have worried. He put in a full ten hours of work and then went to one or another of Dublin's many churches after work, staying there until it was time to go home to bed.

Matt knew he had to avoid his drinking buddies and his pubs in order to put external temptation far from himself. But the internal temptation stayed. He craved alcohol constantly during the first three months of his pledge. The suffering must have been terrible. He told his mother over and over that he was afraid that he would not hold out for the three months of his pledge. He went to Confession every Saturday and to Mass every morning of the week. He worked each day and then spent hours in prayer, asking for the grace to keep his pledge. To remind himself to rely completely on God, Matt put two pins in the form of a cross in the sleeve of the coat that he wore all the time. Whenever he looked at the crossed pins, he remembered his Crucified Savior and said a prayer.

Matt Talbot kept the pledge for forty-one years.

*   *   *

Who was Matt Talbot?

The second son of Charles and Elizabeth was born on May 2, 1856, and named Matthew. Matt was one of twelve children born to the Talbots; only nine survived to adulthood. Charles was a short, thin, strong man who was known for his physical stamina and for the strength of his opinions. He could be hot-tempered and argumentative, and he drank too much. Matt seemed to have inherited his father's physical properties and temperament and his mother's hard-working, generous spirit and strong Catholic Faith.

The country of Ireland was in poor shape during much of Matt's life. Forces of England occupied the country and oppressed the Irish people with terrifying brutality, while keeping the wealth of the country for themselves. The average workingman worked for ten hours a day or more for a wage of only four dollars a week.

Employers paid their employees in cash at a pub of the employer's choice. The workingman was expected to buy drinks with some of the cash that the pub was kind enough to provide for him; if he did not, he could be blacklisted and as a result, would be unable to find work anywhere. The employer or foreman got a kickback of cash from the business generated by this practice. Yet the Faith of the Irish people remained strong, and it was their true wealth.

The family life of the Talbots was a chaotic one. Life became an unending struggle to feed the family and pay the landlord. Home was a few cramped rooms in a tenement building in the poor section of town. Charles and Elizabeth and their growing family moved eleven times in twenty years in an attempt to find affordable housing. In Dublin, it was not unusual for a family of ten or more people to live in a two-room tenement. These rooms had no plumbing or running water of any kind, and residents went to the neighborhood pump or fountain with buckets and jugs to obtain water for their daily use. The rooms were never very warm, and the clothes of the poor failed to keep out the cold.

Matt had very little schooling. He attended a good school run by the Christian Brothers, but did so sporadically. Matt could read but only with great difficulty, and to write anything at all was a real struggle for him. When he was twelve years old, he was considered old enough to work and earn money, so he dropped out of school. His first job was as a messenger boy for a wine merchant. It was at this job that he started drinking.

Charles Talbot drank a lot, and sometimes he drank away his whole paycheck. Elizabeth frequently had to work as a charwoman in order to bring money home to house and feed the family. Unfortunately, Matt followed his father's poor example. He found that it was easy to steal "porter," a kind of wine, from his employers, and on this he was frequently drunk.

The first time Matt came home intoxicated, Charles thrashed him, but it did not change anything. In desperation, Charles got Matt a job on the docks, but there Matt was able to drink whiskey instead! He was paid in cash in his foreman's favorite pub, and he obligingly spent a good deal of his cash drinking there. The pub became his true home, and Matt drank constantly for the next sixteen years.

Matt Talbot loved the drinking life. He had no interest in playing cards, gambling, dancing, sports, or dating. A friend said of him years later, "He was interested in only one thing—drinking."

As a person with a favorite pastime will often do, Matt developed many different strategies to live the drinking life to the full. Sometimes he gave his whole paycheck to the barmaid with the instructions to keep the drinks coming all week. She would tell him when his paycheck was nearly spent so that he would drink slower in order to make the rest of his money last until the next payday. Sometimes Matt pawned his own coat or work boots to get cash for drinks, returning to the bar from the pawnshop coatless or barefoot in the Dublin cold.

Work could be sporadic among the poor of Dublin, so Matt sometimes treated his friends who were short of cash or out of work to drinks. In fact, he was known to be generous in this way because he loved company while he drank, be it his workmates, friends, or his brothers. Matt loved the jokes and storytelling, the arguing for the right, and the companionship of life at the pub. He was well liked and well respected there.

Sometimes Matt even participated in stealing. Many times, Matt and his friends stole a pickled pig's cheek from the bar and sold it for drinking money. Matt was squeamish about being the person to actually do the stealing; in fact, no one remembers him actually doing this, but he was a willing participant in any group effort.

Once Matt and his friends stole a fiddle from an itinerant musician. Stories vary: one says that the fellows simply needed money for drink and stole the fiddle because it was easy to do. Another story says that the fiddler was a wonderful musician and that in their drunkenness, the fellows pawned his fiddle to get money to buy him a drink to show him their appreciation. In any case, the fiddle disappeared into a pawnshop, and the money went around for more drinks.

It is not known if the fiddler ever redeemed his fiddle, because nothing more is known of him. Afterward, when Matt realized what he had done, he felt dreadful and regretted his part in depriving a poor man of the only means he had of earning a living. After Matt took the pledge, he searched for this fiddler for years in order to make restitution to him. Unable to find him, Matt made donations for Masses to be offered for the fiddler's soul.

Matt relied on his father and mother to provide for his meals and housing, rarely bringing any of his pay home to help with family expenses. Once he brought home a few small coins and gave them to his mother.

"God forgive you, Matt," was all she could say.

Matt left the docks and took a job as a hod carrier for a building company. A hod carrier worked at the side of a trained bricklayer, and it was his job to carry the mortar or the bricks on his back to wherever they were needed on the building site. Even though Matt was small and wiry, he was strong and had remarkable stamina. His boss put Matt out in front to set the pace for the other workers because he was so strong and fast. The work was grueling and the pay was meager, but Matt was never heard to complain.

No matter how bad his hangover was, Matt never missed work. He had been away from the sacraments for about three years, but he always attended Sunday Mass no matter how bad he felt. And he was always sure to say a Hail Mary or two before going to bed. Matt Talbot never really lost his Catholic Faith. He just put it aside to pursue the drinking life.

And then he took the pledge.

*　　　*　　　*

Matt Talbot remained faithful to his promise. He was by nature a practical man who was honest with himself. He had no illusions about the work that was cut out for him. He craved alcohol with the intensity of a man who had grown up depending upon it. So he took it day by day. Even so, Matt told his mother and his sisters dozens of times that he feared that he would not make it through the three months of his pledge unscathed. These valiant women redoubled their prayers and sacrifices for him. Each day, he managed to just barely hang on. Finally, having made it through the three months, he took the pledge for life.

Matt's practical mind that had once been so creative in fashioning a comfortable drinking life for himself now devised strategies to keep himself from ever returning to that life and to keep himself on the path to God.

So Matt hid in church. Where else could a poor Dublin workingman go? Instead of going to the pub before work, Matt arose early and said many prayers in his room; then he went to church. Most days, he would arrive at church and wait kneeling outside near the church door for twenty minutes or so until the door was unlocked. Matt waited in all kinds of weather, and nothing seemed to bother him as he knelt waiting and praying. Then he would attend 5 A.M. Mass, remaining on his knees for the entire Mass. When asked about this posture, Matt said that he had read somewhere that kneeling throughout Mass greatly helped a person to concentrate on the Holy Sacrifice; he tried it, found it to be true, and continued the practice.

Grabbing a bite to eat at home—usually a crust of bread—Matt then arrived at work at 6 A.M. He worked as a hod carrier until 5 or 6 P.M. Then he hid in church after work until it was time for bed. At first, Matt used the many churches of Dublin as places in which to hide from the drinking life. Gradually this began to change. Soon he was eager to be in church because he realized that there he was not alone. He was with Jesus in the Blessed Sacrament. The King of Kings and Lord of Lords was Himself present in the tabernacle! Matt loved to be in church with Our Blessed Lord. He had no shortage of prayers to make.

A woman told Matt about her brother who was now living in the United States. She was worried about her brother, because he had told her that he was lonely. Matt could hardly believe it.

"Lonely? With Our Lord always there in the tabernacle where any man can visit Him? Lonely? Sure, that's just plain nonsense!" Matt said to her.

On another occasion, a friend who was in ill health asked Matt's advice on where to find a good doctor.

"Go to the same Doctor I do," Matt replied, "the Doctor always waiting for you in the Tabernacle. Go to Him. Make a visit every day."

Matt prepared for Sunday Mass by going to Confession every Saturday. Matt spent his Sunday mornings in church, often hearing six or seven Masses. After he attended his first Mass, he would come home and recite one of his favorite prayers:

> O good Jesus, accept this Holy Communion as my viaticum, as if I were
> on this day to die. Grant that Thy adorable Body and Blood may be the
> last remembrance of my soul; the sacred names of Joseph, Mary, and Jesus
> my last words; my last affection an act of the purest, the most ardent love
> of Thee, and a sincere sorrow for my sins; my last consideration to expire
> in Thy divine arms, adorned with the gifts of Thy holy grace. Amen.

He then had a bite to eat before returning to church to attend more Masses. He knelt through each one, his back straight, his hands folded in prayer, concentrating completely on the re-presentation of the Passion, the Holy Sacrifice of the Mass, participating with all his heart.

He put up a crucifix on his wall, which he kissed whenever he returned to his tenement room. Under it Matt hung a framed prayer, which he said often. This prayer gives us a window into his thoughts and prayers:

I adore Thee, O most sweet Savior, Jesus, expiring on the cross for our sake. I have no words to express my gratitude for the infinite Goodness Thou hast evinced in dying to redeem me. O Eternal Father, I offer Thee Thy dear Son who hung on the tree of the cross, naked, torn, pierced with thorns and nails, bleeding, anguishing, suffering, expiring. Yes, my God, it is Thine own and only begotten Son I offer to Thee in this lamentable condition; receive His divine sacrifice, accept this offering that I make Thee. It is my ransom. It is the Blood of God; it is God Himself that I offer Thee now, for the payment and acquittal of my debts. I offer Him also for the relief of the Souls in Purgatory, of the sick, the poor and the afflicted, the grace of a happy death for the agonizing, the conversion of sinners, the perseverance of the just, and to impetrate for myself and for those specially dear to me the grace of dying in Thy friendship and love, also the grant of their present urgent petitions. Amen. May the most holy and adorable will of God be ever accomplished in all things. May it be praised forever and ever. Amen.

His decision to no longer carry money was an unusual one. One day early in his pledge, he couldn't stand the thirst for drink any longer. Jingling his loose coins in his pocket, Matt walked into a pub. He stood there, waiting to be served. He waited. And waited. No one seemed to see him. No pub customers looked at him, and no barman, trained to greet each and every customer, saw him or said anything to him. It was as if he were invisible. All of a sudden, Matt realized that this must be the case! God was working a miracle in his behalf to keep him from backsliding. Matt hurried out of the pub as if it were on fire. Down the street he hurried until he came to St. Francis Xavier Church. Entering the church, he stayed there until bedtime, thanking God for his deliverance.

After this, he never carried money. Matt knew that loose change was a temptation for him, and he was willing to put up with the inconvenience of not having money if it would keep him from drinking. He was known to be generous at work, and he gave money whenever anyone asked him to donate to a charitable cause. He now told anyone seeking a donation to come back to see him the next day, when Matt would have the donation ready for them. People were willing to tolerate this idiosyncrasy of his because he was so willing to give. Fortunately, by this time the trade unions had abolished the practice of paying workmen in pubs.

Matt became aware of the reality of evil through personal experience. His sister Mary, seeking to help him, bought a book for him and presented it to him.

"It's for you, to help you," Mary said shyly. She knew that the book was an unusual gift. Matt slowly read the title of the book. It was called *Hell Open to Christians*.

" 'Tis decent of you, Mary, and maybe I need it more than you know," Matt said to her in gratitude. Reading it for the first time "frightened the life out of me," he later told his mother. Heaven and hell were real, and Matt was willing to do whatever it took to avoid hell and attain Heaven. He read this book so often that he had to replace the worn cover.

The Evil One was not happy with this and took revenge on Matt.

Matt was, as usual, kneeling outside the church very early one morning when the door opened, as usual. He'd had a poor night's sleep, so he slowly got to his feet to enter the church. As he walked toward the doorway, Matt felt someone push him roughly with great strength backward and to the side. He reeled and staggered, wondering what person could be so rude, but there was no one there! Matt walked forward again, and again he was pushed roughly backward. Seeing no one again, Matt realized that it was the devil trying to keep him from the help of his Savior. Matt never shrank from a fight. He knew that the names of Jesus and Mary have great power against evil. He backed up, took a running start, and shouted the names "Jesus" and "Mary" as he rushed forward through the church door. This time he went through without opposition.

About two or three years after he took the pledge, Matt had another encounter with evil. It was a Sunday morning, and Matt was at the early Mass at St. Francis Xavier Church. He got up to go to Communion. All of a sudden, he felt utterly overcome with despair. He felt as though all his efforts were in vain, that he would soon return to drink, and that he was already absolutely, eternally damned. He was frozen in place and could not walk forward at all. The feeling was so overwhelming that he finally ran out of the church and wandered the streets of Dublin in a daze.

He found himself in front of the Pro-Cathedral and went in for the 8:00 A.M. Mass. Matt felt better, so again he stood up to go to Communion. But again the overpowering feeling of utter despair overwhelmed him. He ran out again into the street. Finding himself in front of another church, he went in to the 9:00 A.M. Mass, where the same thing happened again.

Matt returned to St. Francis just before the 10:00 A.M. Mass and stood outside the gate on the steps. It was time for extraordinary measures. Matt threw himself down on the ground with his arms extended and lay there in the form of the cross. Sighing from the depths of his soul, Matt prayed out loud for mercy, for the strength to never return to drinking, for Our Lord to deliver him from this and all terrible temptations, for Our Lady to help and pray for him. There were many people nearby waiting for Mass, but no one helped him, or even asked him if he were ill. Perhaps they thought that he was just a disgraceful drunk.

It seemed to Matt as though he prayed for hours like that. In reality, only a few minutes had passed.

Then, just as suddenly as it had appeared, the feeling of despair left him. A feeling of rejoicing replaced it. Relieved, Matt arose and returned to his favorite spot inside St. Francis. Full of gratitude, he received Holy Communion without further incident. Matt had often been drunk in public. Why shouldn't he be repentant in public as well?

Since he had turned so completely away from his drinking life, Matt wanted to make reparation for his misdeeds. After each payday, he went around to the pubs he used to frequent and paid bar tabs on which he still owed money. Some of his friends thought that he paid more than he owed because he would pay any bar tab that anyone told him he still owed, whether or not he really owed the money to the bar. As a result, this repayment process took a long time. He continued to look for the fiddler, but was never able to find him. Matt also made reparation by giving to charity. A frugal man, Matt lived on very little. Whatever money was left over after his living expenses had been paid, he gave to the foreign missions, to the poor, to mission seminaries to help educate future priests, and to a local convent of Poor Clares.

After making amends for his old life, Matt truly embraced his new life. When the Jesuit church where he attended weekday Mass changed its Mass time from 5 A.M. to 6:15, Matt reacted in his customary practical way: he found another job. He went to work for a lumberyard that opened at 8 A.M. This way, he could still get up each morning at 2 A.M. and pray for two hours. Women in his tenement building who were tending sick children remember hearing Matt sing hymns to Our Lady in the middle of the night. He attended Mass at 6 A.M. After Mass, he even had time to make the Stations of the Cross, which was his favorite practice next to attending Mass. He could return home for a bite to eat and then enjoy his walk to the lumberyard, where he began to work at 8 A.M. Matt was happy with the new situation.

It was a rough group that worked at the lumberyard. The men swore a lot. Matt tipped his hat in reverence to the Holy Name whenever he heard a man take it in vain. Noticing this, some men tried to take God's name in vain more often, just to see if Matt really tipped his hat each time—which he did. Gradually, some of the men who were accustomed to swearing stopped the practice because of Matt's good example. When the noon church bells rang for the Angelus, Matt stopped whatever he was doing, made the sign of the cross, and said the Angelus prayers. To the men who ridiculed him for this, Matt only glared, upset at the disrespect paid to Our Lady.

Somehow, though, Matt inspired respect among his coworkers. During breaks in the work, he retreated behind a lumber pile to pray. Knowing this and respecting Matt for it, one man took it upon himself to station himself near Matt and to cough as a signal when someone was coming.

Matt was known as a hard worker who inspired respect in his boss. When a difference of opinion arose, Matt could stand his ground. "With all respect, sir," Matt said to his foreman, "I've never met a man I was afraid of. I fear only God."

Irish labor was in a turbulent state during much of Matt's life. Fed up with low wages, long working hours, and poor conditions, the Irish workers went on strike. Matt was familiar with Pope Leo XIII's encyclical *Rerum Novarum*, which stated that to go on strike was an acceptable way to achieve justice in the workplace when the workers were left with no other alternative. He joined the strike. His union provided a small sum of money as strike pay. Matt seemed to know which of his fellow workers were supporting wives and small children. He gave most of his strike pay to these young, struggling families "to tide you over," as he put it.

At this time there were also uprisings incited by the Irish who were trying to become independent from England. During all this turbulence, Matt spent even more time in church in prayer. Many people believe that it was the prayers of Matt Talbot that finally won a free Ireland for her people.

Matt made changes in his personal life, too. After he took the pledge, he tried to persuade his brothers to stop drinking, but to no avail. He realized that their example could lead him back to the drinking life, so he moved out of the Talbot home and took a small room in a tenement building where he lived alone. One of his married sisters who lived nearby took it upon herself to cook a meal for him and tidy his room each day. This was not much trouble because Matt had little and ate little. He ate his meals kneeling.

One day she noticed some wide boards leaning up against the wall and asked her brother what they were for. He would not tell her. "They're for a purpose," was all he would say.

She soon had an answer to her question. She discovered that Matt slept on them and used a block of wood as a pillow. He searched all over Dublin for a certain statue of Our Blessed Mother holding the Child Jesus. Matt went to sleep clutching this statue in his arms. One of his relatives believed that the pressure from part of the statue each night made one side of Matt's face permanently numb. Matt went to bed at 10:30 P.M., and for years he did not sleep for more than three-and-a-half hours.

Why did Matt live this life of penance? It is true that he imposed all these things as a penance on himself in repentance for his past life; to mortify himself was also a good way to keep temptation far away. But more importantly, Matt did all these things in order to follow a way to holiness. In the early days of his pledge, Matt's spiritual director recommended that Matt follow the rule of the early Irish monks. These monks had lived such lives of great mortification and holiness that they were famous throughout Europe. As missionaries, they had brought the Faith to countless souls. They had found that a life of penance was a true way to holiness, and

Matt imitated them. This rule could be summed up by a quote from St. Columbanus: "Pray daily, fast daily, work daily, and study daily."

After his father, Charles, died, Matt took care of his mother, Elizabeth. She moved in with Matt and lived with him for thirteen years until she died. She cooked and cleaned for him and he supported her. Elizabeth attended daily Mass while Matt was at work. In the evenings, she and Matt prayed the Rosary together; and they loved to recite prayers and litanies and sing hymns together. Matt was reading books again, and Elizabeth loved to hear his stories of the saints, angels, and missionaries. Her new home was a paradise for her. Matt was glad to be able to make up for all the grief he had caused her.

"When I was young, I was very careless about religion because of drink, and I broke my mother's heart," he told a friend years later.

Elizabeth told her daughters that she would awaken in the middle of the night to hear Matt talking to the Blessed Mother as a friend speaks to a friend. Sometimes she would see him praying with his arms outstretched in the form of a cross. His conversion was a great comfort to her until she died.

Matt's eating habits were also worthy of those of a desert hermit. Matt ate very little, mainly bread and vegetables. He received a promotion of sorts in the lumberyard, and managed the stores, or supplies, of the business in a little office. The wife of the caretaker, Mrs. Manning, prepared his beverage for lunch. At Matt's instruction, she poured boiling water into a container, which had unsweetened cocoa and a pinch of tea in it. Matt would wait until this mixture reached room temperature, and then he would drink this bitter beverage.

If Matt were invited anywhere for a meal, he ate whatever was served to him, believing that it was more important to be courteous and charitable than to follow his own preferences. For this reason, few people knew of Matt's penances, and those that knew did not discuss them until after his death.

Matt fasted during Advent and Lent and during all of June because it was the month of the Sacred Heart. He said to a friend, "We do well to punish the body and not be studying the gut." He relaxed his nutritional practices only on Christmas Day when he asked one of his sisters to fry a steak for him.

Matt's manner was modest. He was affable with others, and he always enjoyed a good laugh. He listened much and spoke little. He made a habit of keeping his eyes downcast whenever possible. In this way, he guarded his eyes and ears from occasions of sin. Matt's clothes were very shabby but always very clean. Matt slit his trousers lengthwise at the knees so that he could kneel on his bare knees for extra penance. He wore an old, long coat everywhere, and he wore his cross of pins in its cuff for the rest of his life.

To learn his Faith better, Matt read whatever Catholic literature he could. One day, he read a pamphlet on something called True Devotion to Mary, written by St. Louis de Montfort. It seemed to Matt that this devotion was perfect for the lay state, and for a layman like himself. He decided to follow it with all his heart.

True Devotion was simple. A person wishing to follow it entrusts, or consecrates, himself or herself to Jesus in Mary. He entrusts all his prayers, actions, and virtuous works to the hands of Mary, and promises to do everything in his life through, with, in, and for Mary. In this way, the soul trusts Mary to form him in the image of Jesus. It is a real way of life. St. Louis saw that in the future, evil would abound, and only those consecrated to Mary, those simple and humble, would be able to defeat it.

Matt read two of St. Louis de Montfort's books: *The Secret of Mary* and *True Devotion to the Blessed Virgin*. He made his consecration to Jesus in Mary. Matt's favorite expression became that very one: "To Jesus in Mary." It gave him much to meditate upon. God the Father entrusted His Son to Mary. Shouldn't we entrust ourselves to her so that we can be more pleasing to God? Jesus came to earth only through Mary. Isn't it only right that mankind go to God through Mary, too?

Matt told a friend that True Devotion "lifted me from earth to heaven."

One practice of those following True Devotion is to wear a small chain loosely around the wrist, neck, or waist to symbolize their loving slavery to God. Matt was enrolled in the chain and began to wear one. It was this practice, in a way, that later made him famous.

When Matt met a person who truly wanted to please God, he spoke to that person about his consecration. In this way, he was able to bring many people to True Devotion, and he made many friends this way.

Matt's new life also involved giving money to charity, particularly the missions. Our Lady was always, together with her Son, seeking out the lost. Wasn't he himself the best evidence of that? Since Matt couldn't go to mission fields, he sent money to missionaries to help them with their work. In this way, Matt's workman's life could be as apostolic as that of any missionary. Matt sent donations to Nigeria, China and the Far East, France, and Palestine. He donated to an orphanage in America and helped support convents of nuns. Matt would even sell his possessions in order to donate to charity. A friend was once dismayed to see Matt coatless in the winter cold, since he had given Matt a warm coat to wear. Matt had sold the coat so that he could make a charitable donation!

In order to study his Faith better, Matt borrowed Catholic books from well-educated friends, and he even bought some for himself. Despite his meager education, Matt was able to read and understand some of the most brilliant minds of the Church. He had books by and about St. Teresa of Avila, St. John of the Cross, St. Augustine, St. Francis de Sales, St. Catherine of Siena, Bl. John Henry Newman, St. Therese of Lisieux, St. Peter Julian Eymard, and Blosius, among others. Matt also read many encyclicals of the popes. One of his friends was a well-educated man who wondered how Matt could read and understand such lofty material when he himself found such reading to be challenging.

Matt was glad to explain.

"When I get hold of a book like that, I always pray to Our Blessed Lady; and I believe that she always inspires me to take the correct meaning out of the words," he said. Matt was able to explain the Faith to anyone who had a question about it, and to make the explanation simple and brilliant. For this reason, people sought him out.

One of these people, Ralph O'Callaghan, was so impressed with Matt that he made a lifelong friend of him. One day when Matt was visiting him, Ralph decided to test Matt's humility.

"You know, Matt," said Ralph, "you have been granted great spiritual gifts. But you know there's a danger attached to them; you might take pride in them."

Matt's answer was a model of humility.

"And why would I? The credit isn't due to me, but to God Who gave the grace," he replied. "How little I do compared to all the great saints."

Matt seemed to know the saints as though they were old friends of his. His favorites, understandably, were the great penitents, such as St. Mary Magdalene and St. Mary of Egypt, whom he called "grand girls," and St. Dismas the Good Thief. He loved St. Michael the Archangel and was glad of his help in time of temptation. He had a great love for St. Therese, the "Little Flower," and he thought that St. Teresa of Avila was a "great girl."

To deepen his commitment to God, Matt joined the Third Order of St. Francis and attended its meetings regularly. He joined other spiritual groups, or sodalities, and attended their meetings as well. He was so meek and retiring that many of the people with whom he attended these meetings for years did not know who he was.

But Matt did make a deep impression upon many people.

Monsignor Hickey was the president of Clonliffe College and a good friend of Matt's. The Monsignor thought highly of Matt and told a few people about him and his holiness. "Whenever I wanted a particular favor from heaven, I asked Matt to pray for it. His prayers were never refused," said Msgr. Hickey.

One of Matt's tenement neighbors remembered a young woman who knocked at his door by mistake. She was greatly upset, almost distraught, and told the man that she was looking for Matt Talbot to ask him to pray for her to find a good job. The neighbor pointed out Matt's door to her. Days later, the same young woman knocked at his door, but he did not recognize her, because her face was completely transformed by happiness. She had knocked at Matt's door, but he was not at home. She asked the neighbor to thank Matt on her behalf for his prayers—she had found a new job that surpassed her highest hopes!

Mrs. Manning kept chickens in the lumberyard, and occasionally one of them would lay an egg near Matt's office. She told him that he could keep any egg he found, but Matt always returned the eggs to her. Mrs. Manning's fondest memories of Matt were the times he spent with her children. In his spare moments, he would tell the children stories of saints and angels. He made the stories so vivid that the children almost believed that he witnessed the stories personally. Matt always visited the Manning children on Christmas Day. He would bring the gift of a Christmas coin for each child and then stage an elaborate search through every one of his pockets, "looking" for each child's gift. The children loved Matt's search and looked forward to the tradition each year.

During the Irish Uprising, Matt was "detained," or jailed without reason or charge. The English police forces often rounded up men in groups to see if any were plotting against their government; Matt was part of one such group. He was only held a short time and then released, perhaps because he was an older man at this time and there was no evidence of wrongdoing on his part. But Matt's friends and workmates had lots to say about their various experiences of being beaten, threatened, and detained. They asked him for his story.

"God is so good. Isn't it a pity more men do not love Him?" was all he would say.

On a feast day of Our Lady, Matt confided to a friend that he had assisted at twenty-one Masses in her honor. When his incredulous friend insisted that such a thing was not possible, Matt assured him that it was. With a twinkle in his eye, he explained: "Many Masses were being said at the same time. It is necessary only to have the intention of hearing them all to get the merit of hearing them. Though you're attending only the Mass being offered at the altar before you, you're attending all the others as well." With God, the intention counts for a lot. Matt believed that God accepted this offering, made in good faith.

While walking with Matt, another friend asked if he could smoke. Matt had given up the practice shortly after he stopped drinking, giving away a prized pipe to a startled coworker to avoid temptation.

"Sure," Matt said, bending down. He picked up a small white pebble, dusted if off, and put it in his mouth. "You have yours and I now have mine." He sucked on the pebble as his friend smoked so that the man would not feel uncomfortable smoking alone.

Ned Lyons was distraught that his son Jack was missing and presumed dead in World War I. Matt got wind of it, and he told his friend that his son was all right and that he would be home soon. The man got another telegram saying that his son was dead. "Ned, forget that wire," said Matt. Ned arrived home to find Jack sitting at the kitchen table! He had been given leave to visit home, and his name got on the wrong list.

One of the altar boys of Berkeley Road Church remembered seeing Matt, believing himself to be alone, praying in church before a crucifix, his arms outstretched in the form of a cross. This altar boy was Sean T. O'Ceallaigh, and he remembered:

> Sometimes Matt would be waiting outside before the Church opened for the early Mass. He got to know a few of us altar boys well, and would call us by our Christian names. We always called him Mr. Talbot, although he was very poorly dressed and wore the muffler workingmen wore then instead of a collar and tie. He was very neat and clean; sometimes the boys would call him Holy Joe, making fun of him, but he never resented that. He was very kind and friendly. He would pray aloud sometimes, and seem oblivious to everyone and everything. Later on, when I was older, he often stopped me in the street to ask how I was getting on at school; and when I started work, he would enquire how things were and warn me to mind my work and to do it well.

Sean T. O'Ceallaigh later became the President of Ireland.

Matt went to the hospital twice in 1923, for stays of about a month each. His heart was giving out. Each time, he was given the Sacrament of the Anointing of the Sick, and each time he got better. The second time this happened, Matt recovered slowly. On the first day he was allowed up, he disappeared. The hospital staff looked for him everywhere. Finally, they found him back on the ward. When asked where he had been, Matt replied that he had been in the chapel praying before the Blessed Sacrament. When the nursing sister in charge scolded him for causing such a commotion, Matt smiled. "Since I already thanked the doctors and nurses, it was time to thank the Great Healer," he said to her. His words made a deep impression on her.

The sick benefit that Matt lived on was extremely small. Friends convinced him to accept some charity for himself, and he very reluctantly agreed. He had made a promise to God to wear only old clothes, he said to a priest who brought him some new ones. But it is God Who is giving you these, replied the priest.

Matt finally went back to work in the spring of 1925. He was glad to be back because he did not like to be idle. His coworkers left all of the light work to him because he looked so frail. Matt used his first paycheck to make an offering of Masses in thanksgiving for all the blessings sent to him by God. He knew that his health was poor; in fact, his doctor had warned him that he might die suddenly.

The seventh of June was Trinity Sunday, which was one of Matt's favorite Church feast days. How wonderful to contemplate the Heavenly happiness of the Triune God! Matt began his Sunday as he always did, attending his Masses and saying his prayers. He belonged to the Men's Sodality of the Gardiner Street Church, which had its monthly first Sunday Mass that day, so Matt was sure to attend that Mass with his lifelong friend Paddy Laird. Returning home afterward for something to drink, for it was a hot day, Matt bumped into a neighbor. The man told Matt that he did not look too well; Matt agreed that he felt weak, but he was his usual cheerful self. Matt went into his room, and came out soon after. He told his neighbor that he was going to the church in Dominick Street, and he disappeared around the corner.

As was his custom, Matt proceeded down Granby Lane, which led right to the back entrance of the church. He was approaching the church, when he paused, shuddered, and fell to the ground. Two young men saw what happened and ran to him. Loosening his shirt collar, one of them checked his pulse. He could not find one. One of the men ran to get a priest from the nearby church. When the priest arrived, he saw that Matt was not alive, so he and the men started to pray for the repose of his soul. A doctor who was leaving the previous Mass was called to the scene; he pronounced that Matt had died from heart failure. No one knew who the dead man was.

His body was taken to a hospital mortuary. According to routine procedure, the body was undressed to prepare it for burial, and in cutting away the clothes, the mortician noticed the chains. A chain was wound around the waist, one arm had a chain wound above the elbow, and one leg had a chain wound below the knee to mortify him while kneeling.

Matt's sisters expected him for dinner that night; and when he did not arrive, the panicked sisters reported him missing. The next day, Mary went to the mortuary to identify the body. Even in death, Matt looked serene.

What astonished everyone about Matt were the chains.

Since he had no money, Matt's fellow Franciscans clothed him in a brown habit, and the Men's Sodality of St. Francis Xavier Church paid for the coffin and burial. Appropriately, Matt was buried on the Feast of Corpus Christi, the Body and Blood of Christ. Friends of Matt later put up a beautiful Celtic cross at his grave to mark the spot. This cross was engraved with the Sacred Heart. Matt had urged a friend to have a monument of the Sacred Heart put up in Dublin; this, too, was done. The process for Matt's canonization was opened in 1931.

Matt Talbot continues to inspire people, especially the down-and-out and those who serve them. There is a Talbot Center for the Homeless, a Talbot Food Pantry, and a Matt Talbot Abstinence Program to help those with an alcohol problem. The Twelve Step Program of Alcoholics Anonymous was not inspired by Matt Talbot, but Matt providentially lived out the Twelve Steps many years before they were conceived in the program given to him by the Jesuit Fathers to find sobriety. There is even a Matt Talbot Bridge in Dublin. St. Paul VI greatly esteemed Matt Talbot, as did St. John Paul II, who also greatly desired his canonization.

On June 7, 2000, people from all over the world gathered in Dublin to celebrate the seventy-fifth anniversary of Matt Talbot's death. Present were American Indians from South Dakota who attended in full ceremonial dress; their desire was "to walk the holy ground of the holy man who had a problem with alcohol and used his God to overcome his problem." In his homily, Archbishop Connell said, "The life of Matt Talbot brings new strength to our hope in God. None of us is too unimportant to be noticed by God, none of us so weak as to be beyond his help, none of us so guilty that we cannot recover our innocence by the gift of his forgiveness, none of us so late in starting afresh that we cannot look forward to growing in holiness."

Venerable Matt Talbot, pray for us!

Lesson Activities
Ven. Matt Talbot

Vocabulary

Define the following.

diligent	blacklisted	reparation	apostolic
wary	pawnshop	tenement	meager
pledge	devise	mortification	humility
abstinence	restitution	modest	penitent

Terms to Know

Discover the meaning of each of the following.

1. worth his salt
2. Holy Name
3. Angelus
4. True Devotion
5. Third Order of St. Francis
6. sodality

Comprehension Questions

Answer the following, using complete sentences.

1. What event in his life made Matt decide to take the pledge?

2. Explain what "taking the pledge" means.

3. How long did Matt keep the pledge?

4. How did the threat of blacklisting force a workingman to drink more than he may have wanted?

5. Describe one of Matt's strategies for living the drinking life.

6. Describe one of Matt's new strategies to keep from drinking and to keep going on his way to God.

7. Describe one of Matt's encounters with evil and how he triumphed over it.

8. How did Matt make reparation for his past misdeeds?

9. When someone took God's name in vain, what would Matt do?

10. In what ways were Matt's sleeping habits unusual?

11. How does a person follow True Devotion to Mary?

12. What did Matt say to a friend who wondered how he could read and understand lofty material?

13. What did Monsignor Hickey say about Matt?

14. Matt made an impression on an altar boy from Berkeley Road Church. What was this altar boy's name, and what did he grow up to be?

15. On what feast day of the Church did Matt Talbot die?

16. After he died, what about Matt astonished everyone?

Analyze This

Using as many details as you can, explain each question in paragraph form.

1. How did the labor situation in Ireland encourage vices such as alcoholism?

2. Why did Matt Talbot like the drinking life?

3. After his conversion, what steps did Matt take to avoid going back to the drinking life?

4. How did Matt regard and use money?

5. How did Matt guard his senses to avoid temptation?

6. Why did Matt like True Devotion so much?

7. What kind of impression did Matt make on people?

Essay Questions

Answer one or more of the following in essay form.

1. What influence did the bad example of others have in the life of Matt Talbot?

2. What influence did the good example of the saints have on the life of Matt Talbot?

3. Once he took the pledge, how did Matt change his life?

4. In what ways was the new life of Matt Talbot different from his drinking life?

5. To what lengths did Matt Talbot go in order to follow Christ?

6. How did Matt Talbot practice fraternal charity (love of neighbor)?

7. Why did Matt love Jesus Crucified with such a grateful love?

8. In what ways did Matt practice holy modesty and humility?

9. What motivated Matt to practice such severe penances?

10. What role did Jesus in the Blessed Sacrament play in Matt's new life?

Quotes

Complete one or more of the following.

1. Choose one of the quotes of Matt Talbot. Memorize and recite it.

2. Choose one of the quotes from a person other than Matt. Memorize and recite it.

3. Choose one of the prayers in the story. Memorize part or all of it, and recite it.

4. Reflect upon one of the quotes or prayers in the story in essay form. You may wish to give your essay as a speech.

Geography and History

Complete one or more of the following.

1. Draw a map of Matt Talbot's Dublin, labeling any place names you find in the story.

2. Draw and label a map of Ireland.

3. How did England first come to occupy Ireland? Write a report, outline, or list of your findings.

4. Research and write a report on the labor situation in Ireland during the life of Matt Talbot. Be sure to focus on the situation of the average workingman, and address how the policies and practices of the powerful impacted his life.

5. Research and write a report on the history of the country of Ireland.

6. Research and write a report or speech on how Ireland achieved independence as a country.

7. Research and report on the Catholic Church in Ireland. How did the Church contribute to Ireland's growth as a country?

8. Research and report on the impact that Irish missionaries had on the United States and the world.

Research and Report

Choose one or more of the following topics, and research and write a report about it. Be sure to include related maps, diagrams, time lines, and illustrations.

1. Ireland—past and present

2. Saints of Ireland

3. The history of Irish monks and monasteries

4. St. Louis de Montfort's True Devotion to Mary

5. The Catholic Church and Ireland

6. The Abstinence Movement (or the Temperance Movement)

7. The Twelve Step Program of Alcoholics Anonymous

8. Eucharistic Adoration

You, The Biographer

Research and write a biography of one or more of the persons listed below. Be sure to use at least two sources for your biography. You may wish to present it as a speech.

1. St. Patrick of Ireland

2. St. Louis de Montfort

3. Bl. John Henry Newman

4. St. Catherine of Siena

5. St. Teresa of Avila

6. St. John of the Cross

7. St. Peter Julian Eymard

8. St. Mary of Egypt

9. St. Mary Magdalene

10. St. Francis of Assisi

11. St. Augustine

12. St. Francis de Sales

13. Pope Leo XIII

14. Sean T. O'Ceallaigh

15. St. Therese of Lisieux, the "Little Flower."

Putting Your Faith into Practice

Choose one or more of the following.

1. Matt Talbot had a long list of favorite charities to which he liked to donate. Do some research, and find a reputable charity or missionary group. Earn some money, and send some to your charity. Even if it is a small amount, the recipients will be grateful to you.

2. Select one of the saints mentioned in the story. Find a book by (or about) that saint, and read it to improve your spiritual life. What new insights does it give you?

3. Matt Talbot loved the Mass, seeing it for what it is, the re-enactment of Jesus' redemption of us. Matt knew that at each Mass he was truly present on Calvary with Christ. Choose one of the following to do:

   a. If possible, attend a weekday Mass in addition to Sunday Mass.

   b. Visit Jesus in the Blessed Sacrament, and talk to Him, friend to friend.

   c. Try to concentrate on Mass completely, as Matt did. Gently focus your attention on the words and gestures.

   d. Meditate on the Passion of Jesus. You may wish to use a book, a crucifix, a picture, the Stations of the Cross, or the Sorrowful Mysteries of the Rosary to help you. Do you feel closer to Jesus now?

4. Study one of the prayers in the story, and write an essay or some of your reflections on that prayer. You may wish to give a speech based on your essay.

5. Perhaps you know of someone who conquered a drinking or drug addiction problem. What helped him/her to be successful? If possible, interview this person to find out.

6. Perhaps you know of someone who is still struggling with a drinking or drug problem. Ask Matt Talbot to pray with you for this person. If possible, tell this person about Matt Talbot, his life story, and the power of his prayers.

7. How did Matt Talbot providentially live out the Twelve Step Program of Alcoholics Anonymous? List each of the Steps, and then describe what Matt did to live out each Step.

8. Matt Talbot is often referred to as a "saint for addicts." Define the word "addict," then make a list of your own addictions. These may include over-eating, too much chocolate, TV, computer games, movies, lying, etc. Now develop a plan, as Matt Talbot did, to break your addiction. Remember to fill the "gap" with something positive like prayer time, helping a needy neighbor, and giving of yourself.

St. Josephine Bakhita

Always in the Master's House

Italy: 1930—Convent of the Canossian Sisters

Ida Zanolini took careful notes of what her guest was saying. Ms. Zanolini was a writer, and she was working on a biography of the woman who was now talking. Before her sat a Canossian Sister, dressed in black, wearing a black ruffled bonnet and a large medallion of Our Lady, as all the Canossian Sisters did. The sister was at least sixty years old, but the serenity in her face made her seem much younger. As she spoke, Ms. Zanolini took notes and asked questions, as any good biographer will do. But she felt a growing amazement at the story she was hearing and at the woman who was telling it.

Sr. Josephine Bakhita was from the Sudan in Africa, where she had been kidnapped as a child and sold into slavery. Her life as a slave had been a brutal one. Through an unusual set of circumstances, she had found herself traveling to Italy with the last family to own her; and there she had discovered Jesus Christ, whom she thereafter called "The Master." Desiring to belong to Jesus completely, she had taken vows as a sister and embraced a life of prayer and service.

This life of prayer and service was well known to all. With grace and serenity, Sr. Bakhita did a myriad of household tasks in the convent. She had cooked for the school children and the patients in the infirmary, taught many young women the art of embroidery and beadwork, and served as general doorkeeper for the many people who visited the sisters. Young and old, rich and poor sought her as an advisor and a friend. A person merely had to be in her presence to feel peace and consolation. Her advice was simple and to the point, going straight to the heart of the matter. Sr. Bakhita radiated a holiness of which she herself was totally unaware.

So it was not this life as a sister that her biographer was writing about today; that would come another day. Today, Sr. Bakhita spoke about the tragedy of her capture and her life as a slave. Ms. Zanolini found herself fighting back tears as she worked, listening to Sr. Bakhita's story. As she spoke, tears streamed down Sr. Bakhita's face as she related her memories. She dried her tears calmly and continued telling her story. This part of the story was a tale of cruelty and betrayal, cowardice and greed. How could people be so cruel to one another? How could Sr. Bakhita come through such mistreatment without wanting to take revenge?

Ms. Zanolini commented on how cruel Sr. Bakhita's captors had been and was surprised at Sr. Bakhita's reply.

"I am praying much for them, that the Lord who has been very good and generous to me may be the same to them, so as to bring them all to conversion and salvation," she said.

"Poor things! They were not wicked; they did not know God, or maybe they did not think they hurt me so much. They were the masters, and I was the slave. Just as it is natural for us to do good, so it was natural for them to behave as they did towards me. They did so out of habit, not out of wickedness."

She continued with her characteristic serenity.

"If I were to meet again the slave merchants who kidnapped me and even those who tortured me, I would kneel down and kiss their hands. For if these things had not happened, I would not have been a Christian and a religious sister today."

Here was the secret of Sr. Bakhita's holiness: her Christ-like forgiveness of others and her gratitude for God's blessings, especially the blessing of her Catholic Faith.

*   *   *

Who was Sr. Josephine Bakhita?

Bakhita was born in 1869 in the village of Algoznei (now called Olgossa) in the western part of the Sudan, right in the heart of Africa. The village was a collection of round huts, each of which was thatched with millet and formed part of a large square in which the children played in the daytime and the adults met to discuss village business or to dance in the evenings. She was part of the Daju tribe, which was a ruling tribe of the area. Her uncle was the chief of the village, and Bakhita's family was a very prosperous one. They herded sheep and cattle, and they farmed; the family had so many holdings that they used hired help to care for their livestock and crops.

Bakhita's family consisted of her mother, father, three brothers, and three sisters. The family was close-knit. Her childhood was one of complete happiness. She later said that as a child she did not know what suffering was. Bakhita loved to walk in the forests and meadows, and thorn bushes were her favorites because she often found butterflies in them. She did not know anything about the religious worship of her family, since she was probably too young to be told anything about it; but Bakhita did remember that no one in her village worshipped

idols. Instead, the people of her tribe worshipped a spiritual force that was thought to be present everywhere. Children, the sick, and the elderly were thought to be closer to this spirit-world, and therefore they were given much respect. For the same reason, motherhood was also held in high regard.

Later, Bakhita said, "as a child, when I contemplated the sun, the moon, the stars, and all the beautiful things of nature, I was wondering, 'Who is the master of it all?' And I felt a keen desire to see Him, to know Him, and to pay Him homage."

One sorrow clouded her childhood. One day, her mother wanted to visit their farmland to see if the hired hands were doing their work properly. She planned to take all her children with her, but Bakhita's older sister was not feeling well, so she obtained permission to stay at home with her littlest sister. While they were away in the fields, they could hear the sound of screams coming from the village. When Bakhita's mother and siblings made their way back to the village, they found the little sister hiding in a ruined hut.

She was able to tell them what had happened. Some men she had never seen before came and took her sister: she struggled and screamed, but they took her anyway. The little one hid, and they did not find her—or else they would have taken her, too. Bakhita's mother and the other children searched everywhere, but found no trace of her. When Bakhita's father returned from the fields, they told him what had happened, and he was furious. He, the hired hands, and the village men took spears and shields, and made a thorough search of the surrounding countryside, but no trace of Bakhita's sister was ever found. Bakhita remembered that her mother cried for a long time after that. Bakhita herself never forgot her sister, and thought about her often.

The slave trade was a lucrative one in the Sudan. Arab slave traders would kidnap the young and the strong who could work hard and would bring a good price on the slave market. Since communications were only by word of mouth, the slave traders could escape with their victims with little fear of being punished by the law. The slave trade was officially against the law at that time, but the law was difficult to enforce.

A few years later, the slave traders struck again. We will let Bakhita tell her story:

> One morning, after breakfast, I went out with a friend of mine. I was then about nine; she was twelve or thirteen years old. We walked towards the fields, a short way from home. We stopped playing for a while, and were intent on picking tasty herbs. All of a sudden, two armed strangers crept out from behind a hedge. Drawing near, one of them spoke to my companion.

> "Let this little one go near that bush, and bring me my parcel. She won't be long in coming. Walk along, and she will catch up with you shortly."

> It was clearly their plan to separate the two of us, for, had my friend seen them making off with me, she would surely have raised the alarm. I was too simple to understand their tricks. So I obeyed the man without question, just as I did my mother at home.

> Hardly had I entered the woods in search of that parcel, which was nowhere to be found, than I found those two men right behind me. One of them grabbed me roughly by the arm, while he drew out a big knife from his belt. He poked it against my side, and gruffly commanded: "Shout and you are lost. Quick, follow us." The other man pushed me on ahead of them, the barrel of his gun held at my back.

> I was stunned with terror. Wide-eyed and trembling all over, I tried to scream. A lump in my throat made me dumb. I could neither speak nor cry out. They pushed be on violently, into the thick of the woods. We hurried along hidden paths and open fields.

They marched the rest of the day and all night long. One of the men stole a melon from a field and tossed his prisoner a piece to eat. She was so terrified that she could not even eat a single bite.

"What is your name?" they asked her. The lump in her throat made her speechless, so she did not answer.

"You don't have a name? We'll give you one!" one of the men said, laughing. "We'll call you Bakhita. It means 'The Lucky One.'" They laughed with cruel irony. And so this became her new name. She gradually forgot the name given to her by her family.

In the morning, they arrived at their destination. Bakhita's feet and shins were bleeding from the rocks and sharp grass she had walked across during the night. Her kidnappers threw her into "a hole of a room, littered with tools and scraps." There was not so much as an old burlap sack to serve as her bed. Bakhita had to lie down on the bare floor in almost complete darkness. She stayed in this wretched room for over a month.

> I cannot describe the suffering I went through . . . I still feel the anguish of those hours, when, worn out with crying, I would collapse and lie on the ground in a kind of stupor. My imagination was taking me far, far away, to where my dear ones lived.

> There I would see my beloved parents, my brothers and sisters, I would embrace them all with great tenderness, telling them how I was kidnapped and all I was made to suffer.

> At other times, I imagined I was playing with my friends in our fields. I felt so happy. But all too soon, I was brought back to the sad reality of my awful solitude. Then discouragement would get hold of me, so strongly that it seemed to tear my heart to pieces.

At last, she was released from her prison. The sight of the sun and the sky was almost enough to cheer her up; she was grateful to be out in the open air. But Bakhita was sold to a slave trader. He lined up all his slaves and shackled their necks together, even putting large burdens on the backs of some of the men to carry. Bakhita and another little girl were not shackled, but they walked behind the adult slaves, near the slave trader. The caravan began to march.

The slave caravan stopped at many villages along the way so that the trader could buy more slaves to add to the caravan. The shackles made dreadful, open wounds on the necks of the adults, but never did the slave trader slow down the march nor treat the wounds of his slaves. After eight days, they reached their destination. They were sold to a master, the sickly ones first so that the slave trader would not lose money if they died.

Soon thereafter, their master ordered Bakhita and her new friend to husk some maize. Leaving them in a room of his house, he left to attend to some business and forgot to lock the door!

The girls saw their opportunity. Holding hands, they peered out the door. The coast was clear, so they ran out of the house into the open country. Their hearts light, they rejoiced because they would soon be with their families once again. Running through field, forest, and desert terrain, they ran the rest of the day and during the night.

"We knew that our hope for safety rested only upon the speed of our young legs. For the whole night we ran and ran, into the woods and through desert land. Panting and exhausted, we could hear the roaring of wild beasts, echoing out in the darkness of the night. When the animals approached, the best we could do was to run for a tree and climb it," Bakhita remembered.

Early the next day, as they were traveling, they heard the unmistakable commotion of a

slave caravan. Terrified, the girls hid behind some thorny bushes. For two hours they watched the long caravan pass until it was gone from sight. They were relieved that they had not been captured! Traveling all day, they came to a village as night fell. It seemed to each girl that this must be her home village, but as the two looked closer, they knew that it was not. As they stood there, a man approached them.

"Where are you going, children?" he asked. The frightened girls did not reply, so he repeated his question in a kindly manner.

"We are going to our parents."

"Where do they live?" he asked in the same kindly tone.

"Over there," said the girls, pointing ahead. It did not take long for the man to figure out what had happened.

"Come, take some rest. Then I will accompany you myself," he said. They soon arrived at his home. After giving them some water, the man left, and the girls fell into an exhausted sleep. The man returned in an hour or so and gave them something to eat. Then he took them to the pen in which he kept his sheep, and he put the girls in chains! Distressed at the man's trick and knowing that their hopes for finding their families had been dashed, the girls cried as though their hearts would break.

In a few days, he sold the girls to a slave trader, who walked them to a large caravan. The girls were surprised to see in this caravan slaves who had belonged to the master from whom they had escaped. The slaves told the girls how furious the master had been when he had discovered that the girls had escaped. He had vowed that if he ever found them again, he would cut them to pieces.

"Now I appreciate more and more the kindness of the Lord who miraculously saved me once again," said Bakhita.

The slaves marched for two and a half weeks, chained as they had been before. One poor slave was very sick and could hardly walk. He begged the trader to let him rest, but the trader beat him mercilessly. Crying out, the man collapsed, and the trader beat him still more furiously. He ordered that the man's chain be removed; then the caravan moved on, leaving him behind to die. The other slaves wanted to help him, but they were shackled and could not move freely, so they were forced to move on. The traders had no sympathy for the slaves, and others met the same fate as the poor man. At last, the caravan reached the town of El Obeid. Bakhita and her friend were sold to a rich Arab chief.

The chief was very wealthy and owned many young, strong slaves who worked for him. Bakhita and her friend were assigned to serve the chief's daughters, who liked the girls and were kind to them. The girls were fed and dressed well, and the work they did was not too difficult. The chief intended that the girls would become the property of his son when he got married.

This peaceful interlude was not to last. One day, Bakhita made a mistake that angered the chief's son. In a rage, he began to beat Bakhita, and she ran to the room where the chief's daughters were. This made him still more angry. He beat Bakhita so badly that she could scarcely move. Slaves dragged her to a pallet where she lay for over a month, recovering from her injuries. But her fate was sealed; since the son could not even bear the sight of her, Bakhita and her friend were sold to a Turkish general to serve his wife and mother.

The general's mother thought that the girls were too young to be of any use to them, but his wife said to her, "Don't worry, Mama, we'll train them. They will learn quickly enough— you'll see. What words won't do, the lash will." She showed the girls the whip in her hand and continued, "If we pay a lot of money for a slave, it is so that she can work. In my house those who do not work are starved to death and thrown out to be food for dogs, jackals, and birds. Do you hear?" she shouted at them.

Bakhita went with a senior slave, who showed her a room where many mats lay on the floor. The slave pointed to the mat that was now Bakhita's and gave her some bread to eat. When the other slaves came in for the night, Bakhita was heartbroken that her sister was not one of them. She began to cry. The senior slave threatened her with a whip: slaves were not supposed to cry; and if Bakhita continued, she would be beaten. Bakhita choked back her tears.

In the general's home, slaves were expected to rise at dawn and work until noon. Then they had their first meal, worked all afternoon, and had a scanty supper, worked some more, and then went to sleep on their mats. If a slave became ill or injured, he or she was left on his or her mat and given no care or attention of any kind. When a slave died, the body was thrown in the field or the garbage heap for the animals to find.

Bakhita describe her years in the general's home:

> Another girl and I were assigned to the mistresses, whom we had never to leave for a moment. Between dressing them, perfuming and fanning them, we had no breathing space. Things were not so simple; woe to us if, accidentally, we hurt them. The whip would be on us, without mercy. I can say in all truth that, in the three years I spent in their service, there was not even one day when I was not dealt some punishment or other. When a wound from the whip began to heal, other blows would pour down on me, even though I had done nothing to deserve them.

One day, for example, the general had an argument with his wife. He was so angry that he ordered two of his soldiers to beat Bakhita and her friend as hard as they could. The two girls lay on their mats for two months, recovering from their injuries. In a way, they were lucky, because many other slaves of the household died from these beatings.

Then came one terrible day.

"It was customary for slaves to be tattooed with peculiar pattern designs in honor of their masters. The process would be very complicated, and, naturally enough, very painful. For the marks were done by incisions," recalled Bakhita. The mistress took it into her head that all the slaves not yet tattooed should be made so at once. This would increase her own prestige, as well as bring more money to her if the slave were sold. She called a witch to the house, who came with a dish of flour, a dish of salt, and a razor. She ordered that the three untattooed slaves be brought to her. The first slave was ordered to lie on the ground, with two other strong slaves holding her arms and feet. The mistress stood behind the witch, whip in hand.

"Then, bending over the poor girl, the torturer began to trace on her belly strange patterns with the white flour, about sixty in all. When she had done with the patterns, the woman took the razor and began to make incisions along these, while the wretched victim moaned and bled profusely."

Bakhita watched, horrified. "Salt was rubbed in the wounds, so that the gaping edges of the scars would permanently show off these patterns," Bakhita remembered. The girl was in so much agony that she was carried off, completely unconscious. Then it was Bakhita's turn. Seeing the mistress with her whip stopped any hope of escape. She lay down.

> Six intricate patterns were designed on my breast and sixty more, as was customary, on my stomach, and forty-eight on the right arm. It is hard to express in words what I felt. I thought I would die, especially when salt was rubbed into the wounds.

> Literally bathed in my blood, I was carried away and placed on my straw mat, where I was to remain for several hours, totally unaware of what was going on around me. When I came around, I saw next to me my two poor friends, who had shared the same ordeal. For more than a month, we were condemned to lie down, unable to move, without so much as a cloth to dry the serum oozing from our open wounds. The scars are still evident on my body.

> I can really say that it was by a miracle of God that I did not die, for He had destined me for better things.

Bakhita witnessed and underwent many other tortures in the two following years, but fortunately, her chastity was never violated. "Through the mercy of God, I was preserved," remarked Bakhita. "Our Lady protected me, even before I could know her."

One day, when Bakhita was about fourteen, the Turkish general decided to return to his own country. To do this, he had to sell some of the slaves he owned. Bakhita was part of the group that journeyed by camel caravan to Khartoum. The slaves rested in a hotel there, while word went out that the general had slaves for sale. He asked Bakhita to bring a cup of coffee to one of the guests who came to the hotel to see the general. The man to whom Bakhita served coffee was Callisto Legnani, an agent of the Italian Consul in the Sudan. The man looked at Bakhita intently, but little did she suspect that he was the one who was to buy her—little did she know, it was the beginning of a new day for her.

The next morning, Mr. Legnani's maid came to the hotel. The general ordered Bakhita to help this maid carry a parcel to the Legnani home. When she arrived there, Bakhita discovered that this was her new home! Bakhita had a bath and was given some clean, pretty clothes to wear. When Bakhita served some food to Mr. Legnani, he hardly recognized her. Bakhita herself felt as though she were in a dream.

"This time I was really 'the lucky one'," recalled Bakhita gratefully. "My new master was kind, and before long, he became very affectionate towards me." Mr. Legnani seemed to have known that Bakhita had been badly mistreated as a slave. All those in the household did all they could to make Bakhita feel accepted and loved. Her main duty was to help the maid with the housework. It was light work, compared to the workload she had endured at the general's home. Everyone in the household was kind to her. She was never reprimanded nor punished in any way.

"For the first time since I was kidnapped, I enjoyed peace and tranquility," said Bakhita. She spent two peaceful years in the Legnani home.

One day, Mr. Legnani came home with the news that he had been recalled to Italy. As he made plans for his departure, Bakhita approached him with an unusual request. She asked him to take her with him to Italy. Ever since Bakhita had heard the word "Italy," she had a strong feeling that she should follow her master there. He tried to dissuade her, saying the journey was a costly one and would be a long one, too. But nothing could shake Bakhita's resolve. Finally, he agreed to take her along.

"I now see that it was God who wanted it, although I did not realize this till much later. When I think of it, I can still experience the joy I felt on that occasion," said Bakhita much later.

Accompanying Mr. Legnani was a friend of his, a boy who was a slave like Bakhita, and Bakhita herself. Traveling by camel caravan, the group arrived in Suakin (Port Sudan) and stayed there for a month. The two men received shocking news. After they had left Khartoum, pirates had ransacked their homes and kidnapped their servants. While she was upset at her master's misfortune, Bakhita was grateful that she had insisted that she come along to Italy. If she hadn't, she would have been kidnapped once again.

The group boarded their ship bound for Italy. It sailed up the Red Sea and into the Mediterranean. Mr. Legnani traveled with his friend, Mr. Michieli. By and by, the ship docked at the Italian port city of Genoa. There to meet them was Mrs. Michieli. She took an immediate liking to Bakhita and complained to her husband that he had not brought her someone from Africa to help her with the baby she was expecting. To please his friends, Mr. Legnani gave Bakhita to the Michielis. Much to her regret, Bakhita never saw him again.

When the Michielis' daughter Mimmina was born, Bakhita became her nursemaid. As the years passed, Mimmina came to love Bakhita very much, and, of course, Bakhita loved her back. The family lived in a villa called Mirano Veneto, which was located near some beautiful countryside that reminded Bakhita of home. Mrs. Michieli was more than happy with Bakhita's service. Three peaceful years passed.

Mr. Michieli had returned to the Sudan and was running a big hotel in Suakin. He wrote a letter to his wife, asking her to come to Suakin to help him with his work. So Bakhita, Mimmina, and Mrs. Michieli traveled to Suakin and stayed there for nine months. In that time, the hotel did so well that they decided to remain in the Sudan permanently and make it their home. Since they still had property in Italy, they decided that Mrs. Michieli, Mimmina, and Bakhita should return to Italy to sell the family property and wrap up their business matters there. So back to Italy they went. Even though the Michielis planned eventually to train Bakhita as a waitress to work in their hotel in the Sudan, Bakhita had a feeling that this was not to be so.

"This was to be my last farewell to Africa, my native land. Something in my heart told me that I would never again set foot on its soil," she remembered.

It took two years to settle the Michieli business matters. During this time, Bakhita made a closer acquaintance with Mr. Checchini, who was the administrator of the Michieli property. He was a devout Catholic, and he and his family befriended her. He had several young daughters who became Bakhita's friends, and she was a welcome visitor in the Checchini home.

One day, Bakhita saw a Crucifix in the Checchini house. The sight filled her with a strange feeling. The man on the Cross seemed to be suffering very much, yet he looked full of kindness. "Who are you? Why have they put you on the Cross?" Bakhita asked him softly. Later on, Mr. Checchini told her about Jesus and His suffering and death for us. Even though her command of the Italian language was poor, Bakhita could understand the insults, the blows, the wounds, and the suffering that Jesus had endured.

Mr. Checchini gave her a silver Crucifix on a chain as a gift for her to keep. "When he gave me the Cross, I noticed that he kissed it with great devotion," Bakhita said. "He then explained to me that Jesus Christ was the Son of God and that He had died for us. Naturally, I did not grasp the meaning of this, but prompted by an inner urge, I hid the Cross, afraid that the mistress might take it away from me. Before that day I had never hidden anything from her, nor had I any reason to do so. After all, I owned nothing of my own, nor was I attached to anything. I now remember that, as I looked at the Crucifix, I experienced a strange feeling, which I could not explain."

The time came for Mrs. Michieli to return to the Sudan. In order for Mimmina to receive a good education, Mrs. Michieli took her to the boarding school run by the Canossian Sisters in Venice. It was her wish that Mimmina and Bakhita not be separated, so the two were enrolled in the Catechumenate, which was a school for children who had not yet been baptized. Ordinarily, Mimmina would not have been enrolled there, since she was already baptized, but since the two were to remain together, both were registered at the Catechumenate. Mimmina was five years old and Bakhita was twenty-one.

This was an answer to Bakhita's dearest wish: to learn more about the Man on the Cross. She remembered: "Thus both the child and I were admitted to the Institute. I was entrusted to the Sister in charge of the catechumens, Sr. Maria Fabretti. Whenever I think of the loving care she lavished on me, I feel moved to tears, even now." She continued, "And so the saintly Sisters, with a patience that was truly heroic, instructed me in the faith. They helped me know God, whom I had experienced in my heart since childhood, without knowing who He was."

Learning that He who created all things was indeed her Heavenly Father was a great consolation to Bakhita. Likewise, she was very consoled to learn that Jesus gave His Mother to us in order to surround us with a mother's love and care. The more she learned about Jesus, the more she loved Him. "Had I known the Lord during my long slavery, how much less I would have suffered!" Bakhita commented years later.

Nine months later, Mrs. Michieli returned to Italy. It was her intention to take Mimmina and Bakhita back to the Sudan with her. But Bakhita had already made a decision about her life: she wanted to remain with the sisters so that she could complete her preparations for Baptism. She knew that if she went with Mrs. Michieli, she would have little or no opportunity to practice her Catholic Faith; the family appeared not to practice any religion. Her newfound Faith was the most important thing in Bakhita's life. She would do whatever she must in order to nourish and practice that Faith.

So a young African woman who had never disobeyed an order in her life, nor refused a request, told her beloved owner that she was not going with her to the Sudan. This took Mrs. Michieli completely by surprise. Bakhita had never refused one of her orders. She was genuinely fond of Bakhita and appreciated the care she took of her daughter. She could not imagine her family without Bakhita. As a woman with a temper will do, she exploded in anger, calling Bakhita "ungrateful" for all the good she had done for her.

"But I was firm in my decision: she made a hundred and one pleas but I would not bend to any of them," recalled Bakhita. "It was painful and I felt unhappy seeing her so upset and angry, because I really loved her. I am sure the Lord gave me strength at that moment, because He wanted me for Himself alone. Oh, the goodness of God!"

Bakhita knew the woman well enough to expect a fight, and that is exactly what happened. Mrs. Michieli returned the next day with a woman whom Bakhita did not recognize and made even more angry threats. It was no use, and the two women left angrily. Looking at the Crucifix in the parlor, Bakhita said prayer after prayer that everything would turn out all right.

The superior of the convent appealed to the Cardinal Patriarch of Venice for help, and Mrs. Michieli appealed to the King's Procurator. These two men met to discuss the matter; it was a delicate one, and required delicate handling. They both knew that slavery was illegal in Italy. The moment Bakhita had stepped on Italian soil, she had become a free woman. As such, she was free to decide to do with her life whatever she wanted. They worked out a strategy for telling this to Mrs. Michieli.

The next day, the Cardinal, the Canossian Superior, Bakhita, some of the sisters, Mrs. Michieli, and her brother-in-law, an army officer, met at the sisters' convent. The Cardinal began to explain the situation in detail; there followed a long discussion, which, of course, ended in Bakhita's favor.

"Mrs. Michieli burst into tears—tears of anger and disappointment. Snatching her child, who was clinging to me, unwilling to part, she forced Mimmina to follow her. I was so upset that I could scarcely utter a word. I was in tears myself as I saw them leaving, yet deep in my heart, I felt a great satisfaction and joy that I had not yielded to their threats and coaxing. It was November 29, 1889," Bakhita remarked, carefully remembering the date.

It was the start of her new life.

She continued her preparations, and finally the big day arrived. On January 9, 1890, the Cardinal came to the chapel of St. John the Baptist in the Canossian Catechumenate. He baptized Bakhita, who received the baptismal names Josephine Margaret, and Bakhita (Fortunata in Italian). Bakhita was so grateful for this moment that many times during her life she returned to the chapel to kiss the baptismal font. Here she became a child of God! After the Cardinal bestowed on her the Sacrament of Confirmation, the bells of the Catechumenate rang their approval. He then said Holy Mass, during which Bakhita received her First Holy Communion. We can only imagine her joy.

"Josephine was radiant with happiness," said Giulia Della Fonte, a close friend of Bakhita who lived in the neighborhood. "On her face was no longer that veil of sadness which had been customary to her, but she was transfigured with joy."

There was a crowd of hundreds of people who were trying to squeeze into the small chapel; they had come to share in the joy of this extraordinary young woman. The sisters hosted a reception for the many guests, and Bakhita gave each her customary warm welcome. That evening, Mr. Checchini, who had been present throughout the day, took Bakhita to his home to be the special guest of his family. He was so proud to have been a part of Bakhita's new destiny, and she in turn was grateful to him for helping to bring her to Christ.

Mr. Checchini

For the next four years, Bakhita lived at the Catechumenate, living a life of prayer, study, and service. During this time, Mr. Checchini made her a surprising proposal: he offered to adopt her as a daughter and make her a permanent part of his family. It was a tempting offer, one which Bakhita thought and prayed about. But she refused his offer with her usual gratitude and courtesy. She had been hearing another call in her heart.

"I could hear, more and more clearly, the gentle voice of the Lord, urging me to consecrate my life to Him," she explained later.

Shyness overcame her, so she did not ask if she could be a sister. Yet the call continued. She asked her confessor, and he was very encouraging. "The Lord does not look at the color of one's skin but at the heart that loves Him," he told her. The wise priest advised her to talk to the Mother General of the order, Sr. Anna Previtali. Finally, the two met, and Bakhita asked her question.

"Could a poor African girl be allowed to become a religious?" Bakhita asked Sr. Anna.

"And why not?" answered Sr. Anna kindly.

Bakhita's reply was a shy one. "Until now I have seen only Italian sisters in the convent." Sr. Anna reassured Bakhita, and she left the meeting convinced that her call was a true one. The sisters were very happy when Bakhita applied to join them. Sr. Anna accepted Bakhita into the Novitiate, where she prepared for her upcoming life as a sister by prayer, study, and service. In fact, Sr. Anna was so impressed with Bakhita's holiness that her dearest wish was to personally receive Bakhita's vows as a sister.

It was a happy time for her, but it was not without its difficulties. She still did not know the Italian language very well, and it was only with a great deal of effort that she was able to read even the easiest material that she needed to study. But she persevered, and after a year and a half, she received the habit of the Canossian Sisters. Another year and a half later, she was ready to take her vows.

But first she had to meet with someone. The Code of Canon Law in effect at that time required any person who aspired to the religious life to be evaluated by a prelate of the Church. This meeting was to ensure that no one was coercing the candidate in any way to take the step of becoming a religious. Bakhita met with the new Cardinal of Venice, Giuseppe Sarto, who later became Pope St. Pius X. What a wonderful conversation there must have been between these two saints who both excelled in the virtue of humility!

After listening to Bakhita tell her story, Cardinal Sarto told her, "Take your vows without any fear. Jesus loves you! Love Him and serve Him always, as you have up to now."

Bakhita made her vows of poverty, chastity, and obedience on December 8, 1896. Sr. Anna accepted Bakhita's religious profession herself, just as she had wished. (She died only a month later, grateful that Our Lord had granted this wish.) It was customary for sisters to take new names, but Bakhita kept the ones she received at Baptism. She was Sr. Josephine, or, more usually, Sr. Bakhita. Now she was a Bride of Christ!

On this day, she composed a prayer for all those dear to her:

> O dear Lord, could I but fly southward to Africa and proclaim aloud to all my people Your goodness to me! Oh, how many souls I could win for You! First among all: my dear Mama and Papa, my brothers, my sister—still a slave. . . . I wish I could reach all, all the poor people of Africa. Grant, O Lord, that they, too, may know and love You!

She stayed at the Canossian Convent in Venice for six years, serving Our Lord in doing the housework that was her main duty as carefully as possible. In 1902, she received a transfer to the town of Schio, a beautiful town in the mountains of northern Italy. She was sad to leave her beloved Venice, the place where she had come to know God. But, after kissing the baptistery one last time, she made ready to leave. "After all, we are always in the Lord's house," she said then.

In Schio, the Canossian Sisters served God's people in a myriad of ways. They ran a boarding school for girls, managed an orphanage, taught catechism classes, instructed girls and women in home economics, and actively served in other Catholic associations. Sr. Bakhita's first assignment, one she held for many years, was as a cook in the kitchen.

Seeing an African for the first time, the small children of the school were afraid of her. But she put them at their ease, saying, "Touch me! See! I am made of chocolate!" They licked her hands in order to find out.

Sr. Bakhita quickly became a favorite with them. They would call her "Sister Chocolate," or "Sister Moretta," which means "Sister Brunette."

She became known for her compassionate consideration. For example, she warmed the cups and plates during winter months so that the food served on them would stay hot for the schoolchildren. She prepared the meals for the sisters in the infirmary with special care. Some of the younger sisters were placed in the kitchen with her to "learn the ropes" from her. Sometimes they made suggestions to Sr. Bakhita on how to do things better. Although Sr. Bakhita knew that these suggestions born of little experience would not work well, she accepted them graciously and put them into practice. She taught embroidery and beadwork to the girls in their home-economics classes. Always ready to serve, she later was given a variety of assignments. In 1910, she complied with her superior's request and wrote down the story of her life for the first time.

During World War I, most of the Canossian Sisters evacuated to another location for safety reasons. Sr. Bakhita and a few others stayed behind. The convent was turned into a military hospital, and Sr. Bakhita's days were filled with all the service required to make such an establishment run smoothly. She also served as sacristan, preparing the vestments and vessels for Mass. She spoke freely with the soldiers and officers, addressing them as equals. They, in turn, had a great respect for her. She was not afraid to take them to task when it was necessary. Admonishing them numerous times to stop swearing, Sr. Bakhita got these rough men to improve their language for her sake. She would speak to them about God, referring to Him as "The Master" with such respect that she inspired the soldiers to treat God with greater reverence. She urged all the soldiers to fulfill their Easter obligations, and all but one did!

After the war, Sr. Bakhita served as the doorkeeper of the convent. This gave her an opportunity to be in contact with many people each day. The young schoolchildren looked forward to her warm greeting each morning, and their mothers relied on her as an advisor and a friend. To the many poor people who came to the convent door each day, Sr. Bakhita was respectful and friendly. She listened to their tales of woe with real sympathy and was ready to help anyone. Her own sufferings had made her compassionate toward the sufferings of others.

Sr. Bakhita's religious superiors had another reason for assigning her as a doorkeeper. She was becoming famous. People learned of her story by word of mouth, and wanted to ask her more about her story and receive advice from so extraordinary a person. The virtues of kindness and forgiveness shone from her. Rather that keeping her light hidden, her superiors let Sr. Bakhita shine in her contacts with the public. She was a living testament to the glory of God. Many people reformed their lives after having spoken with her.

Sr. Bakhita knew how to keep all things in their proper perspectives. "When people hear my story, they keep saying, 'Poor thing, poor thing.' I am not a 'poor thing.' I belong to the Master, I am living in His house. It is those who are not wholly the Lord's who are 'poor things.'"

In 1930, Sr. Bakhita's superiors decided to make her story more widely known. The Canossian Sisters are a missionary order, and the wide distribution of her story would renew interest in the missions. So Sr. Bakhita worked with Ms. Ida Zanolini, a professional writer, and the result was a book entitled *Wonderful Story*. It became a best-seller! Now people flocked from all over Italy to meet the Canossian Doorkeeper.

Sr. Bakhita was amazed at the crowds of people that came to see her.

"What are all these people coming here for?" she asked once, as a crowd gathered at the door.

"Why, they are coming to see you!"

This answer amused Sr. Bakhita so much that she burst into laughter that was so infectious that everyone near her had to laugh, too!

In 1935, Sr. Bakhita made a missionary tour of Italy. What did she do? She told her own story. By nature she was shy and reserved, and to speak to large groups of people was difficult for her. "When faced with so many people, I felt as if I was sinking into nothingness," she said about her experience. But she "did it for the missions" at the request of her superiors.

So many people came to hear her that there were often traffic jams in the cities where she spoke. Sr. Bakhita always began her talk by saying, "For God's glory, and in praise of His Providence that brought me to salvation." She always concluded her story with this appeal:

> It is your good fortune to be born in a Catholic country; as for me, I have come to it late. Be grateful to God and Our Lady. . . . Be good, love the Lord, pray for the unhappy souls who do not yet know Him. What a great grace it is to know God!

From 1936 to 1938, Sr. Bakhita was the doorkeeper at the Canossian Convent in Milan. This was the Missionary Novitiate, where women who were going to be missionary sisters studied and prepared. Here she met these young women's parents, who were often reluctant to permit their daughters to become missionary sisters. Speaking with her customary graciousness, Sr. Bakhita often told these parents, "How many thousands of Africans would accept the faith, if only there were missionaries to tell them that God loves them and that Jesus Christ died for them?" Sr. Bakhita was a wonderful recruiter for workers in the missions.

Not long after she returned to Schio, World War II broke out. The Canossian Sisters remained at their convent and did not evacuate this time. Sr. Bakhita's trust in God was complete. When the air raid sirens blared, everyone ran for cover, except for Sr. Bakhita. She continued to do whatever she had been doing, saying: "Let them fire away. It is the Master who is in command." She advised the frightened townspeople of Schio: "Trust in God; if you do so, you treat Him truly as God!"

It seems that the people of Schio knew that they had a saint in their midst. "We have Sr. Moretta with us. She is a saint and she will protect us from disaster," the townspeople would say during the bombings. Bombs damaged only one wing of the town's wool factory, and, miraculously, no one was hurt. This was the only damage that came to Schio from the war! On another occasion, over fifty bombs rained down on the town. Not one of them exploded! The people of Schio attributed their miraculous protection to Sr. Bakhita's prayers. She consoled the many families who had relatives fighting in the war, and she helped the townspeople cope with the Nazi occupation.

In 1943 Sr. Bakhita celebrated her golden jubilee anniversary as a religious sister. For one blessed day, the grateful townspeople of Schio forgot the war and gathered in church to celebrate this anniversary with their beloved "Mother Moretta." The chapel was decorated with flowers and silk hangings as Sr. Bakhita renewed her vows during Holy Mass.

Sr. Bakhita's health began to decline. She suffered from arthritis and asthmatic bronchitis, with recurring bouts of pneumonia. Walking at first with a cane, she soon required a wheelchair. Her fellow Canossian Sisters came to her room, or cell, to comfort her; Sr. Bakhita comforted them instead. "Whenever I entered her cell, even for a short while, I came out of it refreshed, for she took all the consoling words out of my mouth and returned them to me with interest," recalled one sister.

The sisters asked her advice on various matters. She had always been so calm, so one sister asked her, "Have you no passions like the rest of us?" Sr. Bakhita answered, "Of course I have. But when they are really troublesome, I say to them: keep still now, and I'll attend to you later. And then I go on with my work and, by degrees, they just die away."

Another sister asked her, "Don't you ever find religious life difficult?" "Yes! Yes! But I remind myself that the Rule is the Master's own arrangement for us, and that settles the difficulty."

Unable to do any work, she spent many hours in the chapel, adoring her Spouse Jesus in the Tabernacle. She told the sisters: "You go and teach; I will go to the chapel and pray that you may do it well." She realized an important truth: "This is my present occupation: to help one and all with my prayer."

Some of the sisters feared death. Sr. Bakhita told them, "When a person loves another, he desires strongly to be close to the other: therefore, why be afraid to die? Death brings us to God!" They said that they feared God's justice. "Well, let us do now what we would like to have done then. We are now determining our own sentence," she answered wisely.

> I am going slowly, slowly towards eternity. . . . I carry two bags with me: one contains my sins, the other, much heavier, contains the infinite merits of Jesus Christ. When I appear before the tribunal of God, I will cover my ugly bag with the merits of Our Lady. Then, I shall open the other and will present to the Eternal Father the merits of His Son Jesus. I will tell Him: "Now, judge from what you see."
>
> In heaven I will, at least, be able to pray to God for them: my parents who were so good, my slave sister, all Africans, who are so good, but they do not know God.
>
> I am sure I will not be rejected. Then I will turn to St. Peter and say, "You can close the door after me; I am here to stay."

In 1947 she developed a serious case of pneumonia. The doctor said that the end was near. Sr. Bakhita received the Last Sacraments. It was a Saturday, the day of the week dedicated to Our Lady. "I had the fortune to enter the convent on the feast of Our Lady's Immaculate Conception. Today is Saturday; I end my life still with Our Lady. Oh, my Blessed Mother, she loves me dearly," said Sr. Bakhita. Delirious with fever and unable to breathe easily, she said, "The chains are too tight; loosen them a little, please." But the moment passed, and she came out of her delirium.

To a sister who reminded her that it was Saturday, she answered, "Yes, I am so happy. Our Lady, Our Lady!" These were her last words. She died in the evening; it was February 8, 1947. So many people attended her funeral that it was one of the largest that had ever been seen in Schio. Parents put Sr. Bakhita's hands on the heads of their children, asking her to bless them with her prayers.

Sr. Bakhita did not put aside her practice of praying for others upon her death; she answered the many requests for her intercession, and many healings have been attributed to her prayers. On May 17, 1992, Sr. Bakhita was beatified. On February 10, 1993, Sr. Bakhita's remains were returned to the Sudan. On this day, before a huge crowd of Sudanese, St. John Paul II said, "Rejoice, all of Africa! Bakhita has come back to you; the daughter of the Sudan, sold into slavery as a living piece of merchandise and yet still free: free with the freedom of the saints. Blessed Josephine comes back to you with the message of God the Father's infinite mercy."

She was canonized St. Bakhita on October 1st, during the Jubilee Year of 2000, the Year of Reconciliation.

Unfortunately, slavery still exists in the Sudan to this day. Children like Bakhita are still abducted and sold as slaves. Many are found and redeemed, but they carry the physical and mental scars of their enslavement. Muslim extremists in control of the Sudanese government are engaging in a campaign to eliminate the native Sudanese from their homeland. Villages, churches, and schools are bombed. In February of 2000, the Bishop's Holy Cross School was bombed intentionally, and twenty children were killed. Yet the Faith of the people of the Sudan remains strong. St. Bakhita is well known to them, and they rely on her prayers.

St. Bakhita, saint of forgiveness and charity, pray for us!

Lesson Activities
St. Josephine Bakhita

Vocabulary

Define the following.

slavery	villa	consecrate
lucrative	crucifix	occupation (army)
shackle	consolation	jubilee
caravan	transfigured	eternity

Terms to Know

Discover the meaning of each of the following.

Catechumenate

confessor

Superior (religious)

Novitiate

Canon Law

Canossian

Comprehension Questions

Answer the following, using complete sentences.

1. What was Sr. Bakhita's attitude toward those who had held her captive?

2. When Bakhita was sold to Callisto Legnani, her life changed. How was it now better?

3. What happened when Bakhita first heard the word "Italy"?

4. If she had not left for Italy, what would have happened to her?

5. What was Bakhita's main responsibility during her years with the Michieli family?

6. When Bakhita first saw a Crucifix, what did she do?

7. Why did Bakhita refuse to return to the Sudan with Mrs. Michieli?

8. What three sacraments did Bakhita receive on January 9, 1890?

9. Why did Bakhita refuse to become Mr. Checchini's adopted daughter?

10. With whom did Bakhita meet before she took her vows?

11. As a sister, why was Sr. Bakhita so compassionate toward the sufferings of others?

12. When she served as doorkeeper in Milan, what did Sr. Bakhita tell the parents of potential missionary sisters?

13. Why was Sr. Bakhita so glad to die on a Saturday?

14. When was St. Bakhita canonized?

Analyze This

Using as many details as you can, explain each question in paragraph form.

1. When Bakhita was a child in the Sudan, why was kidnapping so easy to accomplish successfully?

2. How did Bakhita think of God when she was a child?

3. How did Bakhita respond to kindness?

4. How did seeing a Crucifix change Bakhita's life?

5. Why did Bakhita want to belong completely to God?

6. What was Bakhita's attitude toward the sacraments?

7. Why did Bakhita agree to go on a speaking tour?

8. In what ways did Bakhita remain unaffected by the publicity surrounding her story?

9. In what ways did Bakhita show compassion to others?

Essay Questions

Answer one or more of the following in essay form.

1. Look up the word "dehumanization." How does the dehumanization of people, such as captured slaves, lead to acts of cruelty?

2. Despite her suffering as a slave, Bakhita later recognized God's protection from worse troubles. What incidents in her life were proof of this?

3. In what ways did Bakhita recognize that God had been leading her to Himself?

4. How did Bakhita develop the virtue of gratitude?

5. How was Bakhita a "saint of reconciliation"?

6. How had Bakhita heard God calling her during all of her life?

7. How did Bakhita's virtues illustrate the equality and dignity of all people?

8. In what ways did Bakhita exemplify the virtue of holy humility?

Quotes

Complete one or more of the following.

1. Find a complete or partial quote spoken by Bakhita in the story. Memorize and recite it.

2. Comment on a quotation from the story in essay form. You may wish to give your essay as a speech.

Geography and History

Complete one or more of the following.

1. Sketch and label a map of the Sudan, using the place names from the story.

2. Sketch and label a map of all the places Bakhita lived and traveled (Italy and the Sudan, as well as the sea routes in between); use the place names mentioned in the story.

3. The Sudan was once a part of the kingdom of Ancient Egypt. Report on the way of life of the people living in the Sudan during ancient times.

4. What is daily life like in the Sudan today? Research and prepare an oral presentation, complete with visual aids.

5. Slavery is still a problem—even in our modern world. Do some research to find out where slavery exists in the world today. Find out what you can about slavery in the Sudan.

6. Today the Canossian Sisters have a mission in the Sudan. Research and find out what you can about missionary efforts in modern Africa. How fast is the Church growing in Africa?

7. Plan an imaginary trip through northern Italy. Research points of interest in both the cities and the countryside. Be sure that your itinerary includes the places where St. Bakhita lived.

Research and Report

Choose one or more of the following topics, and research and write a report about it. Be sure to include related maps, diagrams, time lines, and illustrations.

1. The Sudan—Yesterday and today

2. The Canossian Sisters

3. The Catholic Church in Africa

4. Ancient Sudan and Egypt

5. Italy and World War II

6. Modern slavery and the redemption of slaves

7. St. Magdalen of Canossa

Putting Your Faith into Practice

Choose one or more of the following.

1. Find out more about present conditions in the Sudan and how you can help the people there. Do some research, and find organizations that assist the Sudanese people. Write to one of these organizations, asking what you can do to help.

2. St. Bakhita's forgiveness of her tormentors is truly Christ-like. Reflect on one or more of the following:

    a. Consider the example of Jesus on the Cross, forgiving those who crucified Him. How have the sufferings that they inflicted upon Him merited grace, forgiveness, and glory for us?

    b. How would our world be different if nations and groups forgave one another?

    c. What steps can I take to make the forgiveness of Christ shine more brightly in this world?

    d. What can I learn from the example of St. Bakhita, and how can I be more like her?

3. St. Bakhita went about her duties quietly and conscientiously. She saw each duty as the will of God for her at that moment, and she abided peacefully in that "will" by fulfilling those duties. How can you imitate her in your daily life?

4. St. Bakhita had a great appreciation for the sacrament of Baptism. Make a pilgrimage to the church where you were baptized, if this is possible, and offer God a prayer of thanksgiving for this great grace. If it is not practical to visit your baptismal church, then compose and say a prayer of thanksgiving for your Baptism. You may wish to compose your prayer as a poem.

For more information:

Sudan Relief Fund
P.O. Box 7084
Merrifield, VA 22116-9798

Canossian Daughters of Charity
5625 Isleta Blvd. SW
Albuquerque, NM 87105

Pope St. Pius X

To Restore All Things in Christ

Venice, Italy: 1903

Cardinal Sarto could hardly believe how many people had gathered to wish him farewell. They lined the canals and hung over the bridges, waving and shouting or nodding and smiling, as the gondola in which he rode made its way to the train station. The people of Venice never failed to surprise him, mused Giuseppe Sarto. What a bother they were making over him—he, who was only a poor postman's son. The fact that he himself was a cardinal never ceased to amaze him.

He loved the people of Venice, and they in turn loved him back. But such a fuss! After all, he was only going to Rome, probably for only a short stay. Although he was a cardinal, he was in the habit of giving away to the poor any money he had, and so Cardinal Sarto had to borrow money for the round trip train ticket to Rome. He knew he would be back soon, and then he would pay the money back. He always did.

Cardinal Sarto disliked pomp in any form, and often went about in disguise. Just recently, he had traveled to pay a pastoral visit to a convent of nuns. Afraid that there would be a big commotion made at the station, he had telegraphed to a friend that two priests who did not know the area would be arriving by train. Would he send a carriage to meet them at the station? the Cardinal asked. Of course, replied the friend, who accompanied the rickety carriage to the station himself. To his surprise, the two priests he greeted as they stepped from the train were Cardinal Sarto himself, dressed as an ordinary priest, and a priest companion!

"A blessing! A blessing!" shouted the people of Venice. Smiling, the Cardinal blessed them.

How different the splendors of Venice were from his home countryside of Riese, he mused to himself. Small towns, good farmland, warm people, and much poverty. Riese was his home, but now he seldom had the opportunity to visit there. That was why he was grateful that two of his sisters kept house for him; it was almost like being at home. He remembered how sad his sisters had been when he left for the station.

"Maybe you won't come back," they said, tears in their eyes.

He did his best to reassure them that his stay would be brief. He convinced his sisters to take a short vacation in the country, and he told them that he would meet up with them there on his way back to Venice from Rome. They worked too hard, he had told them fondly, and they needed the change of fresh air.

The crowd grew louder and more numerous as Cardinal Sarto neared the station. Once he arrived at the station, they broke out in a loud ovation. It seemed as though each person wanted to touch his hand, to wish him well, to receive his blessing. The Cardinal was overwhelmed, and with tears in his eyes, he spoke to them.

"Thank you for this wonderful demonstration of love," he said. This brought fresh cheers.

"Another blessing! Another blessing! Who knows if you will ever come back!" shouted the crowd.

"Alive or dead, I will come back," he joked with a smile.

With a final blessing and a wave, he boarded the train. As it pulled out of the station, he gazed out the window at the city to which he expected to return. Little did he know, it would be his last sight of Venice.

Giuseppe Cardinal Sarto was a man of contrasts. He was a man of the people, having been born of peasant stock. He had enormous strength and vitality, getting along well on only four hours of sleep a night. When he was not working, he was studying far into the night. "Work is man's chief duty on earth," he loved to say, and he took on projects that would daunt a younger and fitter man. He was at ease among everyone and could bring out the best in both the great and the small. He was a man of strong faith and a deep, burning love of God that shone forth in his every word and deed. His zeal for God was contagious, and many people attributed their renewed faith to his good example and his kindness.

Cardinal Sarto was very intelligent, and he owed his education to the scholarships that he earned by applying himself diligently. All he had wanted to be was a simple country priest, serving his people, but gifts like his could not be kept hidden. He was repeatedly promoted against his will, as he rose through the ranks to become Patriarch of Venice.

The reason for his trip to Rome was a simple one. Pope Leo XIII had died. This great man had been the Servant of the Servants of God for over twenty years; he was affectionately known as "the workingman's pope," for his inspired and progressive social teaching. He had been an excellent teaching and pastoral pope. He would be a difficult man to follow, thought Cardinal Sarto; and silently he said a prayer, asking God's guidance on the task that lay ahead.

For it was his task, together with the other cardinals who were arriving in Rome from throughout the world, to elect a new pope. Cardinal Sarto prayed for the guidance of the Holy Spirit in the decision they all faced.

He arrived at Lombard College, where he had arranged to stay with his secretary, Monsignor Bressan, and his valet. While waiting for the conclave to start, he visited with old friends and made some new ones.

A French journalist asked him if he spoke French. Answering in Latin, Cardinal Sarto replied that he did not. He understood written and spoken French perfectly, but he thought that his accent was too poor to speak it well.

"Ah, then, if you do not speak French, then you are not eligible for the papacy," remarked the journalist. At that time, French was considered to be the "international language," since it was used in the field of diplomacy and international relations.

"Thank God, no," answered Cardinal Sarto, "I am not eligible for the papacy."

Cardinal Sarto did not mean this literally, but he did have reason to say this. For many years, the men who had been elected pope had been men who had served in Rome for many years, who knew the intricacies of diplomacy and procedure. They had been brilliant, well-educated men, but most importantly, they had been men of great faith and holiness. Cardinal Sarto was far too humble to regard himself as an equal of such men.

But unknown to him, many were impressed with his reputation and his pastoral care of his people. And of course, his own holiness shone like a beacon. Meeting him for the first time, many of the cardinals came away gratified at the experience. One person described him as ". . . a man of God who knew the unhappiness of the world and the hardships of life, and in the greatness of his heart wanted to comfort everybody."

The cardinals gathered in seclusion in the Sistine Chapel. Each sat in a stall with a small desk in front and a small canopy above. The procedure for electing a pope is a simple one. After attending Mass and receiving Jesus in the Holy Eucharist, the cardinals vote. Each cardinal writes on a piece of paper the name of the man whom he wishes to be the next pope, and each then places his vote in a chalice on the altar, saying the oath as he does so. This is the oath:

> I call to witness the Lord Christ, who will be my judge, that I am electing the one whom before God I think ought to be elected.

After being counted, the ballots are read aloud. If no one person receives two-thirds of the votes, then the ballots are burned with a small amount of damp straw. This makes black smoke, a sign to the outside world that the cardinals have voted but no pope has yet been elected. Voting takes place twice a day, morning and evening, and each voting session is called a "scrutiny." When the voting results in one person receiving a two-thirds majority, the ballots are burned alone, making white smoke, a sign to the world that "we have a Pope!"

At the first scrutiny, Cardinal Sarto received five votes. This surprised and troubled him. This number doubled at the second and quadrupled at the third scrutiny. He was in utter anguish.

"I am unworthy, I am not qualified. Forget me!" he said, addressing the cardinals.

Cardinal Gibbons of Baltimore remembered this unforgettable scene. "It was that very adjuration, his grief, his profound humility and wisdom, that made us think of him all the more; we learned to know him from his words as we could never have known him by hearsay."

Another unforgettable scene happened at the third scrutiny. Showing obvious signs of embarrassment, the Cardinal of Krakow read a letter from Austrian Emperor Franz Joseph, expressing his desire to veto the possible election of Cardinal Rampolla, who at that time had the greatest number of votes. This veto had no power, and it was not legally allowed; but from time to time rulers sought, though unsuccessfully, to sway a papal election. Those present said later that this unfortunate incident had no bearing on their voting. Still, the votes for Cardinal Sarto kept increasing at each scrutiny.

Deeply distraught, Cardinal Sarto spent long hours in prayer. The cardinals had each been given a room so that they could remain in seclusion for the duration of the conclave. Many cardinals visited him in the small room that he had in the building. They urged him to accept should he be elected. It is difficult to comprehend the anguish that must have seized him during this ordeal. Praying before a crucifix, he reflected that Jesus had himself experienced great anguish in the Garden of Gethsemane and had given all he had to save us. Could he himself give all he had, even his own will? No, not alone, but with God's help, and in union with Jesus, he could.

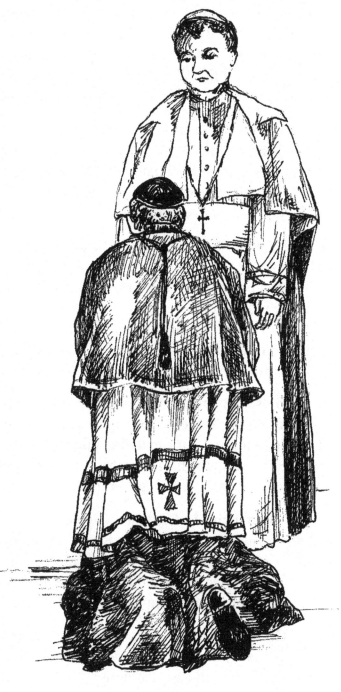

On the morning of the fourth day of the conclave, Cardinal Sarto received more that the two-thirds majority of votes.

"Do you accept?" came the official question.

"I accept," he answered.

"What name will you take?"

"I will be called Pius," he answered.

The ballots were burned, and all the canopies over the cardinals' stalls folded down all at once, except one.

He was dressed in white, and the papal ring was placed on his finger. He went to the balcony and blessed the crowd, which was so happy that he was their new pope. He was well loved in Italy but not well known in the rest of the world. Yet word of this great pastor of souls soon spread throughout the world. The cardinals had chosen well.

It was time to "receive the obedience" of all the cardinals. One by one, each cardinal knelt before the new Pope, and each offered him his full allegiance, support, and prayers. Afterward, Giuseppe

Sarto went to his room and remained praying before a crucifix. His valet tried several times to persuade him to eat something, but it was as though he had not heard. After a long time, he turned to his assistant, Monsignor Bressan. "Come, it is the will of God," he said simply.

This humble man would change history.

*   *   *

Who was Giuseppe Melchior Sarto?

He was born on June 2, 1835, in the village of Riese, in the district of Venice. His father was Giovanni Sarto, a man who wore many hats: he was a cobbler, the city messenger, the caretaker of City Hall, and the town postmaster. His mother was Margherita, a woman of strong faith who was a dressmaker by profession. The Sarto family was very poor, very large, and very close-knit. What they lacked in material resources, they made up for in hard work, determination, resourcefulness, and a vibrant Catholic Faith.

Giuseppe—he was called Bepi at home—attended the village school. He loved to serve at Mass, and by the time he was twelve, he was the head altar boy in his parish church. That same year, he made his First Holy Communion, which was customary in those days because it was thought that a child any younger was not ready to do so. Giuseppe's First Communion was a very special event for him.

He was an excellent student and had a natural aptitude for the catechism lessons taught by the priests of his parish, Don Fusarini and Don Orazio. These two priests noticed Giuseppe's ability, and one of them took it upon himself to tutor him in Latin so that he would be able to go on for more schooling. So Giuseppe went on to the school at Castelfranco, which was four miles from home. Family finances were tight, so Giuseppe walked to school barefoot, carrying his shoes slung over his shoulder in order to make his shoes last longer. After school, there were always farm chores to do with his brothers and sisters.

Giuseppe had been hearing a call to the priesthood for a long time now. His parents could not afford further schooling for him, so with the help of Don Fusarini and Don Orazio, he applied for a scholarship to the seminary at Padua. Giuseppe was a brilliant, hard-working student, and he knew that life at the seminary would require dedication and self-discipline. He was ready and eager for whatever the future might hold.

Fortunately, the Cardinal of Venice was himself a son of peasants, as Giuseppe was, and had also come from the town of Riese. He approved a scholarship for Giuseppe. The Sarto family was overjoyed at the news. Fifteen-year-old Giuseppe went on to Padua, where, as always, he excelled at his studies. He developed a great love for the Holy Bible and the writings of the Church Fathers—a love that would deepen over the coming years.

One sorrow clouded his seminary days. He asked permission of his superior to go home one day because he had some kind of premonition that his father was deathly sick. Permission was granted, and Giuseppe returned home to see his father one last time just before he died of a sudden illness. That same day, Margherita gave birth to a baby boy who died shortly thereafter.

Heartbroken, Giuseppe offered to leave the seminary, come home, and support the family, since he was the oldest living son. Margherita would not hear of it. Vocations to the priesthood were precious gifts from God that must not be squandered. It is the responsibility of everyone in the Church to support and nurture these vocations, especially the family members of those who were given these vocations. She would manage, she told Giuseppe, and she did.

Giuseppe Sarto was ordained to the priesthood on September 18, 1858 at the age of twenty-three, at Castelfranco, where he used to walk to school barefoot. His first priestly assignment was as a curate, or assistant priest, in the town of Tombolo. The pastor, Don Antonio Costantini, was an intelligent and devout man; but unfortunately, he was very ill and was often bedridden. As a result, he was not often able to serve his parishioners as he would have liked.

Don Sarto leaped into this breach with his customary energy, and he made the visits to parishioners that Don Costantini was not able to make. When Don Costantini was sick, Don Sarto would nurse him, while taking on all the duties of the older priest as well as his own. Don Sarto learned a great deal from his superior; and they spent many hours in the empty church, Don Sarto practicing his sermons and Don Costantini giving him helpful suggestions. Both priests shared a love of the Bible and the Church Fathers, as well as a love of good music.

Don Costantini esteemed the good qualities of his curate. He wrote to a friend: "They have sent me a young man as a curate, with orders to form him to the duties of a parish priest. I assure you, it is likely to be the other way about. He is so zealous, so full of common sense and other precious gifts that I could find much to learn from him. Some day he will wear the mitre—of that I am certain—and afterwards? Who knows?"

The people of the parish soon grew to love and esteem Don Sarto. Since he was so easy to talk to, they would share their problems with him. There had been much political upheaval in their district in the recent past. The government had tried to control religion and education by attempting to eliminate them altogether, believing that a population that was ignorant and irreligious was easier to control. As a result, schools and parishes had been understaffed or closed for many years. Nearly a whole generation of people had little or no education at all. Some of the adults bemoaned their lack of education and wanted to learn to read and write. Don Sarto established a night school for these adults, and he taught them himself; he even persuaded the schoolmaster to help.

In return for his time and efforts, Don Sarto had in mind a certain form of payment, but he waited for his students to ask him what it was. One day, they did. "Don Sarto, you work so hard teaching us, and you do this for nothing. What can we do to repay you?" Don Sarto had his answer ready. "Stop swearing. If you do that, I will be more than repaid." The people, adults and children alike, could scarcely hold a conversation without swearing, and this had bothered Don Sarto from the start. So his parishioners made a real effort to stop swearing for his sake.

He was also bothered by the fact that his parishioners scarcely knew or understood their

Catholic Faith. He knew that ignorance of the Faith leads to ignorance of morals and honorable conduct and that the result would be a community unraveling at the seams. "Most of the evil in the world comes from a want of the knowledge of God and of His truth," Don Sarto liked to say. To combat this ignorance, he taught catechism to adults and children, encouraging his parishioners to learn their Faith well enough to teach the Faith themselves. His parishioners took his zeal for the Faith to heart and began to share his apostolic spirit.

He even began a singing school. Anyone who wanted to learn to sing Gregorian Chant at Mass was welcome to join. Soon he had a choir that was the envy of many parishes. Don Sarto deplored the music of the day that was heard in many churches; it sounded as if the singers were in an opera singing contest, and there were too many musical instruments, each one trying to outdo the others. He knew that Chant, with its roots deep in the past—some scholars believe that a form of Chant was sung in the Temple in Jerusalem in Jesus' day—was the most prayerful form of music. He proved to many skeptics that average villagers could learn to sing it, and sing it well.

Don Sarto tried to imitate Christ in every way, especially in his attitude toward the poor and toward poverty itself. He gave away any spare money he had to the poor. Poor people knew this, and they approached him at all hours and in all circumstances. When he preached at a neighboring parish, poor people would ambush him as he left because they knew that he would give his preaching stipend to them. And if he became aware of a poor boy that had a vocation to the priesthood, Don Sarto would tutor the boy himself.

At the age of thirty-two, in 1867, Don Sarto was transferred to the parish in Salzano as its pastor. At this new parish he did many of the same things he had done in Tombolo. He concentrated on Catholic education, offering classes in the catechism for young and old alike and quickly becoming a favorite of the parish children. So many people from neighboring parishes came to Don Sarto's catechism instructions that the other parish priests complained to the bishop. Quoting Scripture to them, the Bishop said, "Go thou and do likewise." Don Sarto also promoted the singing of Gregorian Chant and formed another choir school to teach his people to sing it well.

Don Sarto continued to practice holy poverty, giving away all he had to the poor, even the food in his house. His sister Rosina kept house for him, and one day she told him, "There is nothing for dinner."

"Don't we have a couple of eggs?" he asked. So it was an egg dinner that day.

Don Sarto established a savings bank for farmers to help them improve their situations, and he sought to teach them better ways to farm. He was tireless in his efforts to help the poor in any way he could.

Rosina told an old friend who was visiting, Don Carlo, that Don Sarto had received a small sum of money recently. His clothes were threadbare, and he really needed some new shirts. Could Don Carlo persuade her brother to buy some fabric from the peddler who would visit tomorrow? When the man arrived, Don Carlo examined the linen, negotiated a fair price, and had the shirting cut. Turning to Don Sarto, he said, "Pay up!" A disgusted Don Sarto reached into his pocket and paid up. "Even you come here and plot to betray me," he told his old friend. Later a delighted Rosina thanked Don Carlo: "If you had not been here today, tomorrow there would have been neither money nor linen!"

In 1872, an epidemic of cholera swept through the district. It took a dreadful toll on the people, and many lost their lives. Don Sarto seemed to be everywhere. He visited the sick, gave Last Rites to the dying, and comforted families who had lost loved ones. Many of the sick became somehow convinced that the medicine given to them by the doctors would make them die more quickly. They would take the medicine only if Don Sarto gave it to them himself; this he did, and he did much to reassure the sick. The epidemic was so dangerous that the victims had to be buried at night, and no one was allowed to attend the funerals for fear of catching and spreading the disease. Don Sarto even carried caskets and dug graves himself, and he performed the burial rites of the Church for each deceased person. He wore himself out during the epidemic and was never to regain all of his former vigor.

In 1875, Don Sarto received another promotion. He now wore three hats: he served as the chancellor of the Diocese of Treviso, a canon of the Cathedral, and the spiritual director of the seminary. His greatest love was the care and training of future priests, and he devoted himself to the care of the seminarians with all his energy. He taught them a regular course on meditation and instruction so that they would be well grounded in their Faith. He helped poor seminarians; and when one of them would get ill, Don Sarto would take care of him. Without telling anyone, he would use his small stipend to buy warm cloaks for the seminarians. He would even teach First Communion catechism lessons to the young boys at the school there.

These young men studying for the priesthood took to Don Sarto like steel to a magnet. He seemed to have a real gift for inspiring the young with a real love of God. Yet Don Sarto was the life of the party during the daily recreation period at the seminary. Although he always carried a sheaf of papers with him because of his many duties, at recreation he would put these aside. He had a rule: no serious topics during recreation. If a student mentioned the word "logic," he was obliged to tell a funny or interesting story.

In 1884, Don Sarto was summoned to meet with his bishop, Monsignor Appolonio, who asked him to kneel with him before the Blessed Sacrament and pray for a matter that concerned both of them. After their prayer, Monsignor Appolonio gave Don Sarto a letter from the Pope. Don Sarto had been appointed Bishop of Mantua. Don Sarto wept. He was not worthy, he said, the position was beyond him. He was gently urged to accept by his Bishop, who told him, "It is the will of God."

He accepted and was consecrated Bishop of Mantua. He seemed to have a genius for accepting the unfathomable will of God and finding his peace within that will. He visited his elderly mother and said to her, "Mamma, look at the ring they have given me." Bishop Sarto held up his hand with its new Bishop's ring. His mother was equal to the challenge. "Yes, but you would not have that ring if I did not have this one!" Smiling, she held up her hand, showing him her wedding ring. She knew that the family is the true seedbed of vocations.

The Diocese of Mantua was a place full of problems. The local government had been hostile to the Church for many years. It had taken over Catholic institutions, such as hospitals, orphanages, and schools; closed others; and levied crippling taxes on anything owned by the Church. The local government was trying to drive the Church out of existence. Of course, this had not happened, but the Church was in a very weakened state as a result of this persecution by the government. Seminaries, the training ground for future priests, were nearly empty. Many churches had no resident priest. The priests themselves were poorly prepared, and they neglected teaching the catechism to their parishioners. The religious habits of the people of Mantua had become very lax.

Bishop Sarto dedicated himself to remedying these problems. In his first pastoral letter read to all in his diocese, he said:

> I shall spare myself neither care nor labor nor watchfulness for the salvation of souls. My hope is in Christ, who strengthens the weakest by His divine help; I can do all in Him who strengthens me! His power is infinite, and if I lean on Him it will be mine; His wisdom is infinite, and if I look to Him for counsel I shall not be deceived; His goodness is infinite, and if my trust is stayed on Him I shall not be abandoned. Hope unites me to God and Him to me. Although I know I am not sufficient to the burden, my strength is in Him. For the salvation of others I must bear weariness, face dangers, suffer offences, confront storms, fight against evil. He is my hope.

The first thing he worked on was the seminary. Within a year it was brimming with young men studying for the priesthood. Bishop Sarto even sold some land he had owned near his boyhood home of Riese in order to pay the expenses of feeding, clothing, and educating these young men. Inspired by the bishop's self-sacrifice, others were moved to donate generously to the seminary.

Bishop Sarto visited mayors and other political leaders, disarming all of them with his enthusiasm for saving souls. He also began a newspaper. Not content with this, he founded many schools and even organized a system for teaching the catechism to students who attended public schools, where all religion was banned. In an effort to educate adults, he insisted that his parish priests teach the catechism to the people during their sermons at Mass. And, as he had done so many times before, Bishop Sarto regularly taught catechism lessons to the children himself.

He was a great believer that a bishop needed to visit all the parishes in his diocese on a regular basis, so he began a regular round of visits. He disliked pomp in any form: "I desire no useless pomp, but rather the salvation of souls," he liked to say. He insisted that there be no grand reception when he arrived. Rather, he wanted the people to assemble in the church for Mass with him. This would go a long way to benefit the eternal souls of the people. He also made it his routine to hear confessions everywhere he went. Seeing the importance their Bishop put on the sacraments, the people of the diocese returned to the practice of their Faith in great numbers. Under Bishop Sarto's care, the Diocese of Mantua was transformed into a diocese strong in the Faith.

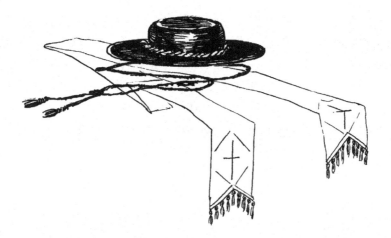

Gifts like his needed a wider scope, so in 1893 he was consecrated Cardinal of the Diocese of Venice. Since he had continued to donate all his extra money to the poor, he had to borrow money for the train trip to Rome for the ceremony to receive his red hat. Because of political problems, he could not assume his new duties for sixteen months; but when he finally did, the people of Venice welcomed him gladly.

The Diocese of Venice had problems similar to that of Mantua. Again, the reason for these problems was the political situation. The government prohibited all religious teaching in school. Charities run by religious groups had been taken over by the government, which did a much poorer job in serving the needy. The government even stepped in and confiscated all the money donated to charitable groups, keeping it from the very people it was meant to serve and help. God was being ruthlessly driven out of society.

The results were devastating. In the Diocese of Venice, as at Mantua, seminaries were nearly empty, priests were scarce, the people hardly knew the basics of the Faith, and there was great poverty. In his first pastoral letter to his people, Cardinal Sarto wrote:

> God is driven out of politics by this theory of the separation of church
> and state. He is driven out of learning by systematized doubt; from art
> by the degrading influence of realism; from law by a morality which is
> guided by the senses alone; from the schools by the abolition of religious
> instruction; from Christian marriage, which they want to deprive of the
> grace of the sacrament; from the cottage of the poor peasant, who disdains
> the help of Him who alone can make his hard life bearable; from the
> palaces of the rich, who no longer fear the eternal Judge who will one
> day ask from them an account of their stewardship. . . . We must fight this
> great contemporary error, the enthronement of man in the place of God.
> The solution of this, as of all other problems, lies in the Church and the
> teaching of the Gospel.

Cardinal Sarto began with the seminary, and then he began to visit parishes. He celebrated Mass and heard confessions at the parishes he visited. He insisted that parish priests teach the basics of the Faith from the pulpit and that they themselves give good example by being hard-working, tidy, and clean. When Cardinal Sarto visited a parish, he often behaved more like an ordinary priest than a Cardinal of the Church. One priest who was late found Cardinal Sarto already hearing confessions in his church! He also visited the sick, bringing the Blessed Sacrament to them—and many ill people were surprised and pleased to find the Cardinal himself at their bedside. He visited people in prison and in the hospital; and he made a regular habit of visiting convents, schools, and anywhere priests, brothers, and nuns served his people.

He brought the focus of the people back to Jesus in the Blessed Sacrament. In 1898 he held a Eucharistic Congress in Venice, the first gathering of this kind to be convened in many years. This congress was held in reparation for the many sacrileges committed against Jesus in the Blessed Sacrament; and parishioners from every church in the diocese participated, attending conferences and missions preached on the Eucharist. On the second day of the congress, he spoke to the people:

Jesus is our king, and we delight to honor as our king Him whom the world dishonors and disowns. We, His true subjects, offer our true homage to Christ the King; the warmth of our love shall be greater then the coldness of the world. We meet around the tabernacle where Jesus remains in our midst until the end of time; there faith springs up anew in our hearts, while the fire of His charity—the very fire that He came to cast upon the earth—burns within us. The object of this eucharistic congress is to make reparation to our Lord Jesus Christ for the insults offered to Him in the Blessed Sacrament; to pray that His thoughts may be in our minds, His charity in our institutions, His justice in our laws, His worship in our religion, His life in our lives.

On the final day, there was a Eucharistic procession through the streets of Venice. All the people dressed in their best, and the bishops, cardinals, and patriarchs wore their most splendid vestments. It was an unforgettable event.

Cardinal Sarto promoted the use of Gregorian Chant and did much to improve the quality of church music. This was difficult in Venice, where the people were greatly attached to loud, operatic singing and complicated instrumentals, but he succeeded in making great strides.

Some of his accomplishments were practical ones. He supported various charities, often pawning his ring to raise funds for them. In one region, he revived the art of lace making. The area was very poor, but in the past it had been a prosperous center for the manufacture of handmade lace. Only one old woman was left who knew how to do it, and he convinced her to teach others. This grew into a small business, which attracted more women. Cardinal Sarto encouraged the enterprise; and before long, six hundred women were working at this lost art.

He even supported organized labor. When the Workingman's Society was organized in Venice, Cardinal Sarto paid the dues and became its first member. He urged people to vote and let their views be heard, and he led a prayer crusade during election time. He mediated disputes between labor and capital, and he was skillful in reaching solutions acceptable to both sides.

His personal habits remained simple. His two sisters cooked and kept house for him, and he continued his lifelong habit of poverty and simplicity in everything. He visited his mother, clad in the red of a cardinal.

"Bepi, you are all red!" she exclaimed with a smile.

"And Mamma, you are all white!" he exclaimed, gesturing toward her white hair. It was truly unusual for a mother to see her son become a cardinal, and Margherita was thankful for this honor. She died not long after, and Cardinal Sarto was always grateful for the Faith that she taught him with her words and her life.

Then in 1903, Pope Leo XIII died, and Cardinal Sarto journeyed to Rome for the conclave.

*   *   *   *

Pope Pius X chose his motto from the epistles of St. Paul: "To Restore All Things in Christ." People sensed that this man was a truly holy Pope, and they flocked to his audiences in great numbers. To people who called him "Papa Santo" (the holy Pope), he replied, "You have one consonant wrong; I am 'Papa Sarto'."

They began to applaud after his sermons. But this new Pope forbade any applause in St. Peter's, saying: "It is not fitting that the servant should be applauded in his Master's house."

He did not want to change his own personal style of living when he became Pope; some things he was able to change, while others he could not. Learning that the Pope traditionally eats all his meals alone, he changed this immediately. Often he made do with just some cheese and nuts for a meal. Yet some of his habits had to change: his secretaries had to remind him not to wipe his pen on his sleeve, since now he wore papal white instead of the black cassock of a priest or bishop.

A Vatican official approached him to ask which titles of nobility he wished to bestow on his sisters; this, too, was an old tradition. "The Lord has made them sisters of the Pope; that should suffice," he replied. He, as well as his sisters, had always chosen the more simple, humble way, and he saw no reason to change that now. His sisters lived nearby, and they had places in his private chapel and at every important Church gathering; they were more than content merely to be near their brother. "Thank God, we are all able to support ourselves," one sister said, "we need trouble him for nothing. Poor dear, he has all the poor people in the world to think of now."

Still, becoming Pope was quite an adjustment. "Look how they have dressed me up," he said to an old friend while wearing all his regalia. The friend noticed that he was nearly in tears. He said to another friend: "It is indeed a penance to be forced to accept all these practices. They lead me about surrounded by soldiers like Jesus when he was seized in Gethsemane."

He went to work with his usual energy. His diplomatic style was direct and candid. One of his first acts was to abolish forever any political influence in any future papal elections. The government of France confiscated Church property, from the largest church to the smallest residence of a country priest, and sought to regulate all use of it. This policy was taken to extremes. Vandals came to country churches and stole and smashed whatever they liked; and police came with them to protect their "right" to do this, while the people looked on helplessly! Rather than deal with a hostile government at every turn, Pope Pius X sacrificed Church possessions. Some people thought that this was foolish, but the Pope had a view of the future in mind. Referring to those who objected to his decision, he said, "They are too concerned about material goods, and not enough about spiritual." Many in France supported his action. Monsignor Gauthey, the Bishop of Nevers, said: "Pius X, at the cost of sacrificing our property, emancipated us from slavery. May he be blessed forever for not shrinking from imposing that sacrifice on us."

His uncompromising actions on behalf of the purity of the Faith inspired a whole generation of young men to seek the priesthood. These young priests were ready for any sacrifice, wearing their poverty and deprivation like a badge of honor. These vigorous young clergy were instrumental in renewing the Catholic Faith in France. Too, there was no longer any political interference in appointing bishops, and this gave the Church a wider scope for action.

This "simple country priest" turned out to be a skilled diplomat. The Pope strenuously objected to the poor treatment of Indians who worked on rubber plantations in Peru. He encouraged mission efforts to serve these Indians. When he issued a teaching encyclical on St. Charles Borromeo, German Protestant leaders misunderstood certain passages and objected to the document. The Pope had done nothing wrong, but he knew how to be charitable. He explained the passages in question in the Vatican newspaper, *L'Osservatore Romano*, and told German Bishops to downplay the document for the sake of keeping the peace.

The Pope went a long way to combat a heresy known as Jansenism. Originating in the 1600s, it was a collection of beliefs that masqueraded as a higher form of Christianity, but in reality it was diabolic in origin. Jansenism portrayed God as harsh and vengeful, punishing every misstep. Holiness was only for a chosen few, and the Sacrament of the Eucharist was a reward for the virtuous, not a help for the faithful. If a person dared to receive Holy Communion without first being a great saint, that person was thought to have committed a grave offense. The results of this heresy were devastating. Many average people, fearing that holiness was completely beyond their grasp, made little effort to live good Christian lives. People received Holy Communion only once or twice a year. Priests tended to stress condemnation and punishment in their sermons, rather than the kindness and mercy of God. The love of God had grown cold.

"Holy Communion is the shortest and surest way to Heaven," said the Pope. "There are others, innocence, for instance, but that is for little children; penance, but we are afraid of it; generous endurance of the trials of life, but when they come we weep and ask to be spared. Once for all, beloved children, the surest, easiest, shortest way is by the Eucharist. It is so easy to approach the holy table, and there we taste the joys of Paradise."

He took action. He lowered the age at which children could receive Holy Communion to the age of seven, the age of reason. He urged the faithful to receive Holy Communion daily, if possible, and he also made it easier for sick people to receive the Eucharist.

"The primary purpose of the holy Eucharist is not that the honor and reverence due to our Lord may be safeguarded, nor that the sacrament may serve as a reward of virtue, but that the faithful, being united to God by holy communion, may thence derive strength to resist sinful desires, to cleanse themselves from daily faults, and to avoid those serious sins to which human frailty is liable," wrote Pope Pius X in his decree. Union with Christ was indispensable in the life of faith. "Frequent and daily communion, as a thing most earnestly desired by Christ our Lord and by the Catholic Church, should be open to all the faithful of whatever rank and condition of life, so that no one who is in the state of grace, and who approaches the holy table with a right and devout intention, can be hindered therefrom."

He changed the face of the Church overnight. People began to come to Communion at Sunday Mass, and what had once been a trickle became a torrent. Average people now attended weekday Mass on the way to work, students attended in school and college chapels, and people in mission fields received Holy Communion often. Morals and conduct improved. Holiness was within the reach of everyone. And most of all, young people became close to Jesus while they were still unaffected by the world.

He invited to the Vatican all the children who made their First Communions in the parishes of Rome, and he spoke to them and personally interacted with them. Some French children came in pilgrimage to thank him for lowering the age for First Communion. As he walked among them, speaking to them and asking them questions, the children asked the Pope to cure and convert their friends and relatives. The children sensed his kindness and the greatness of his heart. So in awe of him were they that some of them answered his questions with "Yes, Jesus."

A woman, who visited with the Pope in a private audience, brought her four-year-old son with her. As she spoke with the Pope, the boy played in another part of the room. He came up to the Pope, put his hands on his knees, and looked intently up into the Pope's face. Pope Pius was charmed and gazed at the boy kindly. "How old is he?" he asked the boy's mother.

"He is four; and in two or three years, I hope he will receive his First Communion," the woman replied.

As he looked earnestly at the boy, the Pope asked him, "Whom do you receive in Holy Communion?"

"Jesus Christ," the boy answered promptly.

"And who is Jesus Christ?"

"Jesus Christ is God."

Turning to the boy's mother, the Pope said, "Bring him to me tomorrow and I will give him Holy Communion myself."

Pope Pius X also combated Jansenism through a myriad of reforms. He founded a biblical institute for the study of Scripture under the direction of the Jesuit fathers; and he commissioned the Benedictines to revise the Latin Vulgate, which was the most accurate translation of Scripture and remains the Church's official version. The Pope went far to encourage daily Scripture reading by all of the faithful. He reformed the Divine Office, which is the daily prayer of the Church, and gave his reforms of Church music a wider scope. He even encouraged the inclusion of modern music in the Mass, provided it was appropriate. He began a revision of Canon Law; and he reformed most of the tribunals, offices, and congregations of the Holy See.

He urged all priests and bishops to teach the catechism to all the people—even people otherwise well educated often were surprisingly ignorant of the basics of the Faith. Encouraging every parish to provide catechetical teaching to all of its members, the Pope himself preached every Sunday in a Vatican courtyard on that day's gospel; anyone could attend. To a lady who asked him what she could do for the Church, the Pope replied, "Teach the catechism."

Another erroneous belief, the heresy of Modernism, had crept into the beliefs of people and destroyed the faith of many. Modernism denies all beliefs but its own, teaching that there are no absolutes, no unchanging realities; rather, the only reality is a person's own private consciousness or sentiments. According to this heresy, everything is relative; we can know nothing for certain but our own reactions to things; faith is not a divine gift but a personal feeling; truth is whatever a person decides it is. Further, Modernism teaches that Jesus is not the son of God and that the Bible is a collection of stories which are probably not true. In claiming to "modernize" the Catholic Faith, Modernism in reality sought to destroy it completely.

Pope Pius X combated this heresy of Modernism by his decree, *Pascendi Dominici Gregis*. In this document, he outlined the errors inherent in Modernism and gave practical remedies for its elimination. He mandated that all priests take the "Oath Against Modernism." As always, his actions had their critics, but most saw that he sought to purify the Church. Thanks to his efforts, this pernicious belief withered away, and the Catholic Faith was greatly strengthened. (Unfortunately, it resurfaced many decades later and troubles us again today.)

"He had the greatest heart of any man alive," said a person who knew him well. Pope Pius X could not hear about suffering without trying to relieve it himself. He also knew that good teaching would inspire others to be generous with their money and their time. Social action was always one of his main concerns; and by his teaching, the Pope urged that Christian principles be applied to the social problems of the day. This inspired a generation of young people to put their Catholic Faith into action, and in so doing, to try to reform society. As always, the Pope put his teachings into practice. Upon being consecrated Pope, he directed that alms be given to several thousand poor people. When Messina was hit with a devastating earthquake, he spearheaded relief efforts himself. In fact, he took it upon himself to support from his own pocket four hundred children who had been orphaned by the earthquake. He undertook so many charitable actions that people wondered where the money came from. "God will provide," he liked to say.

It was said that the prayers and the touch of the Pope had healed people. Inspired by these stories, a girl in England decided to go to Rome to be healed. Her head and neck were covered with dreadful sores that nothing could heal. The girl read in the Acts of the Apostles that the shadow of Peter cured all those it fell upon. Pope Pius X was the successor of St. Peter. Perhaps the Pope could cure her.

The girl and her mother traveled to Rome and attended a public audience of the Pope. As he walked among the people, the girl knelt, and the Pope blessed her. Immediately, she felt as though she was cured. When her mother later removed her bandages, the sores had completely disappeared.

Two nuns from Florence also decided to travel to Rome to meet the Pope. They were both suffering from the same incurable disease and had made the trip to Rome with a great deal of struggle. The taxi driver who transported them to the Vatican felt pity for the sisters who looked like they would die at any moment. At a private audience, they asked the Pope to cure them. "Why do you want to be cured?" he asked them.

"That we may work for God's glory," answered the sisters.

The Pope placed his hands on their heads and blessed them. "Have confidence, you will get well and will do much work for God's glory," he told them. With that, the nuns felt that they were cured. The Pope asked them to keep silent about what had happened. But they both looked so well and walked so strongly that they did not look like the same women. Their cab driver did not believe that they were the women he had brought, refusing to take them back to the convent at which they were staying. "No, I will take back the two I brought or their dead bodies," he said.

"But we are the two you brought," insisted the nuns, but this did not convince him. "No, the two I brought were half-dead," said the cab driver. "You are not in the least like them."

A man brought his little son to a public audience of the Pope. The boy had been paralyzed from birth and had never even stood up. Seeing him, the Pope was moved with compassion. "Give him to me," he said to the boy's father, who handed him to the Holy Father. Pope Pius held the boy on his knee while he talked to a group of pilgrims. After a few minutes, the boy crept off the Pope's knee and began to run and play in the room.

A small boy of two was very sick with meningitis, and his doctor told the heartbroken young parents that there was no possible hope for the boy's recovery. They refused to give up hope. "We will write to the Pope! We used to go to Confession to him at Mantua when we were children," they said to the doctor. "Bishop as he was, he used to hear the confessions of the poor." They wrote and sent the letter. The Pope not only read the letter, he wrote a reply to the couple, telling them to pray and hope. The boy recovered completely the very next day!

In the summer of 1914, Archduke Franz Ferdinand, the heir to the throne of the empire of Austria-Hungary, and his wife were assassinated in Sarajevo. Nearly all of the countries of Europe marshaled their forces for the war that would be known as the Great War, the most terrible war up until that time. The Pope did all he possibly could to forestall this terrible conflict, to no avail. To the representative of Austria-Hungary who asked him to bless their army, the Pope replied firmly, "I bless peace, not war."

"This war will be the death of me," he said to those close to him. Indeed, he offered his life so that war could be averted. He ceased to smile. When he got sick with bronchitis in August, not even his doctor was worried. But in a few days he got worse, and by the nineteenth, the bells of the churches in Rome began to toll for a pope in his death agony.

The Pope could hardly speak. "I resign myself completely," were his last words. He recognized those who came to his bedside, silently clasping their hands. From time to time, he made the sign of the cross. At 1:15 A.M. on the morning of August 20, he died. "The Holy Father died of a broken heart," said one person, and it seemed to many that this was true.

His will was an astonishing document. "I was born poor, I have lived poor, and I wish to die poor," he had written. Pope Pius provided for his valet, sisters, nieces, nephews, and for the four hundred orphans of the Messina earthquake. Monsignor Benson wrote, "Pius X has left his mark on the world." He was buried in St. Peter's Basilica. He was canonized in 1954 and was the first pope to be canonized in 342 years. So that he could keep his promise to the people of Venice, St. Pius X's body was transferred to Venice for a month in 1959.

Lesson Activities
Pope St. Pius X

Vocabulary

Define the following.

gondola	allegiance	seminarian	uncompromising
ovation	catechism	counsel	heresy
daunt	vocation	conclave	audience
pastoral	apostolic	enthronement	forestall
adjuration	cholera	suffice	bronchitis

Terms to Know

Discover the meaning of each of the following.

1. Cardinal
2. Bishop
3. Empire of Austria-Hungary
4. Church Fathers
5. Gregorian Chant
6. Eucharistic Congress

Comprehension Questions

Answer the following, using complete sentences.

1. Cardinal Sarto had been promoted against his will all his life. What did he really want to be?

2. Why did Cardinal Sarto travel to Rome?

3. Cardinal Sarto received twenty votes at the third scrutiny. Addressing the cardinals, what did he say?

4. Just before and just after he accepted his election as Pope, where did Pope Pius X pray?

5. Giuseppe Sarto came from a poor family. How was he able to attend the seminary at Padua?

6. Don Sarto was an assistant priest in Tombolo. What did he do for the adults who wanted to learn to read and write, and what payment did he request?

7. Finish this quote of Don Sarto: "Most of the evil in the world comes from . . ."

8. Don Sarto tried to imitate Christ in His attitude toward the poor. Give at least one example of this.

9. Don Sarto devoted himself to the care of seminarians. Give at least one example of this.

10. The Diocese of Mantua was full of problems. What was the main reason for these problems?

11. When Bishop Sarto visited the parishes in his diocese, he wanted no grand reception. What did he ask the people to do instead?

12. In 1898, Cardinal Sarto held a Eucharistic Congress in Venice. Why?

13. When the government of France confiscated church property, Pope Pius X sacrificed it. How did his action help the Church in France?

14. Pope Pius X took action to combat the heresy of Jansenism. What three changes did he make?

15. What did Pope Pius X do to combat Modernism?

16. Pope Pius X undertook so many charitable actions that people wondered where the money came from. What did he say?

17. Finish this sentence: It was said that the prayers and the touch of the Pope . . .

18. After trying unsuccessfully to stop the Great War, Pope Pius X died on August 20, 1914. What did many think was the cause of his death?

Analyze This

Using as many details as you can, explain each question in paragraph form.

1. Why did Cardinal Sarto think that he should not be Pope?

2. What made Cardinal Sarto finally change his mind and accept his election as Pope?

3. In what way did his family's poverty cause hardships for Giuseppe, and how did he overcome them?

4. Why did Don Sarto stress the teaching of the catechism?

5. Why did Don Sarto encourage the singing of Gregorian Chant?

6. In what ways did Pope Pius X care for the sick during his life?

7. In what ways did Pope Pius X remain close to his family?

8. Why did Pope Pius X value the Eucharist so highly?

9. How was Pope Pius X zealous for truth and right?

10. How did Pope Pius X practice holy simplicity during his life?

Essay Questions

Answer one or more of the following in essay form.

1. Why did Pope Pius X have such an enormous influence on the people around him?

2. Pope Pius X suffered many hardships during his youth and young adulthood. How did this form his character and foster the virtue of compassion in him?

3. In what ways did Pope Pius X, as priest and later as Bishop, endeavor to improve the spiritual lives of his parishioners?

4. In what ways did Pope Pius X, as priest and later as Bishop, try to improve the material (or temporal) lives of his parishioners?

5. How did Pope Pius X practice the virtue of Christ-like poverty all his life?

6. How did Pope Pius X show in his life how much he cared for the souls of young people?

7. How was Pope Pius X a good pastor of souls?

8. How did Pope Pius X lean on Christ for strength?

9. How did Pope Pius X practice the spiritual and corporal works of mercy?

10. In what ways did Pope Pius X show that the Holy Eucharist was central to his life, a life of faith?

11. How did Pope Pius X combat Jansenism?

12. How did Pope Pius X practice compassion?

13. How did Pope Pius X live out his motto: To Restore All Things In Christ?

Quotes

Complete one or more of the following.

1. Choose a quote from the story. Memorize and recite it.

2. Choose part of a quote from the story. Memorize and recite it.

3. Comment on a quote from the story in essay form. You may wish to give your essay as a speech.

Geography and History

Complete one or more of the following.

1. Research and draw a map of Italy, labeling all the place names from the story.

2. Research and draw a map of the city of Rome, being sure to include Vatican City.

3. Research and draw a diagram of the Sistine Chapel or of St. Peter's Basilica.

4. Research and write a short report on the City of Venice. Be sure to include a map.

5. What was the Empire of Austria-Hungary? Research and write a short report to find out; be sure to include a map. What modern countries did this empire encompass?

6. Research to learn how to read and use Roman numerals, and give an oral report based on your findings.

Research and Report

Choose one or more of the following topics, and research and write a report about it. Be sure to include related maps, diagrams, time lines, and illustrations.

1. Italy in the 1800s—Its Changing Political Situation

2. The Persecution of the Church by European Governments

3. How a Pope is Elected

4. The Holy See

5. The Ceremony for Consecrating a Bishop

6. The Ceremony for Consecrating a Cardinal

7. The Causes of World War I—The Great War

8. The Worship of the Holy Eucharist

9. Gregorian Chant

10. The Divine Office

You, The Biographer

Research and write a biography of one or more of the persons listed below. Be sure to use at least two sources for your biography. You may wish to present it as a speech.

1. Pope Leo XIII

2. Cardinal Gibbons of Baltimore

3. Emperor Franz Joseph

4. Archduke Franz Ferdinand

5. St. Benedict, founder of the Benedictine Order

6. St. Ignatius of Loyola, founder of the Jesuit Order

7. St. Anthony of Padua

Putting Your Faith into Practice

Choose one or more of the following.

1. Locate and read Pope St. Pius X's "Oath Against Modernism." Reflect or write upon one or more of the following:

    a. How has reading this document enlightened and strengthened your faith?

    b. Modernism has re-surfaced in our time. How have you noticed its beliefs? What can you do to keep your own faith strong?

2. Pope St. Pius X gave generously to the poor in many different ways. In what way can you imitate him? Outline a plan to give time, money, items, food, or prayers to help the poor; then carry out your plan.

3. Pope St. Pius X is known as "The Pope of the Eucharist." How can you deepen your love for Jesus in the Holy Eucharist? Here are a few suggestions to get you started:

    a. obtain a good prayer book, and look up prayers to Jesus in the Eucharist. Some prayer books contain prayers that are surprisingly rich in content. Use these prayers before or after Sunday Mass, or during a Eucharistic visit.

    b. find out where and when there is Exposition of the Blessed Sacrament. You may need to call local churches, convents, or monasteries to find out. Attend Exposition, and adore Jesus in prayer, using your own words. Tell him of your thoughts, dreams, concerns, hopes, and faith in Him.

    c. help a child or adult who is preparing to receive his/her First Holy Communion. You may wish to teach prayers to him/her, help him/her learn the catechism, or just discuss the sacrament with him/her.

4. Pope St. Pius X encouraged vocations to the priesthood. How can you imitate him? You may wish to pray for vocations, make a visit to a seminary, make a donation to a mission seminary, or encourage someone you know to consider the priesthood.

5. Pope St. Pius X knew how to care for the sick. Take a course in First Aid, or take a nursing assistant training course. Learn how to do CPR. These skills could come in handy some day.

6. Pope St. Pius X loved to pray before a crucifix. Imitate him, and think about Christ's passion as you do so. Does this bring you closer to Him? Does it help you to understand His heart? You may wish to make a cross or crucifix from materials found in your geographic area, such as wood, vines, branches, fiber, or other plants.

7. Note the Pope's shield on the bottom of page 95. Research the symbolism. Now draw or make a shield that depicts your own "motto" for life!

For more information:

The official Vatican website

www.vatican.va

Answer Key to

Reading Comprehension Questions

St. Katharine Drexel

1. Their names were Bishop Martin Marty and Fr. Joseph Stephen.

2. They were missionary priests from the West, and they requested funds to build and run Catholic schools for Indian children.

3. It left most of them poorer that ever and without schools for their children.

4. Accept any reasonable answer, including: They were devout Catholics. They were wealthy yet generous to the poor. They believed in a good education for their daughters. They were close and loving.

5. Kate finished her schooling when she was about twenty, and she was "introduced into society."

6. No, she was not, but she kept trying.

7. Accept any reasonable answer, including: Original sin brought suffering and death into the world. Bringing souls to Christ is the most important work anyone could do. The only thing that consoles Jesus is the saving of souls. Faith alone matters. It would be good to become a nun.

8. "Why not, my child, yourself become a missionary?"

9. She entered the convent of the Mercy Sisters in Pittsburgh in 1889 to learn the religious life.

10. The states were: Oklahoma, Montana, Wisconsin, North Dakota, South Dakota, Wyoming, Idaho, Washington State, and California.

11. "You have no time to occupy your thoughts with that complacency or consideration of what others would think. Your business is simply, 'What will my Father in Heaven think.'"

12. This school is called Xavier University.

13. Most black children of the bayou had one month per year of schooling, or none at all.

14. Mother Katharine built twenty-four schools for black children of the bayou, and she hired Xavier University graduates as teachers.

15. Mother Katharine could pray all day before the Blessed Sacrament, just as she had wished in the days of her vocation search.

16. Accept any reasonable answer, including: She prayed for everyone; she left no one out. She prayed for the children in her missions and for all those suffering during World War II.

Ven. Matt Talbot

1. When Matt was broke, he expected his friends to treat him to a drink; instead, they avoided him.

2. The only way for an alcoholic to conquer the hold that alcohol has on him or her is to promise never to drink again.

3. Matt Talbot kept the pledge for forty-one years.

4. Employers paid employees in cash at a pub, where employees were expected to buy drinks. To refuse to do this was to risk being blacklisted.

5. Accept any reasonable answer, including: Matt gave his whole paycheck to the barmaid so he could drink all week. Matt pawned his coat or boots to get cash for drinks. Matt treated others to drinks because he loved company. Matt participated in stealing to get money for drinks.

6. Accept any reasonable answer, including: Matt hid in church. Matt rose early and prayed. Matt went to morning Mass every day. Matt remained kneeling throughout Mass. Matt worked long hours. Matt went to Confession each Saturday and to many Masses on Sunday. Matt treated his crucifix with reverence. Matt never carried money. Matt gave to charity.

7. Choose one: a. When entering church one day, Matt was pushed backward by an invisible force. He took a running start, shouted the names of Jesus and Mary, and overcame it. b. Matt was overcome with despair. After wandering from church to church, he lay down in the form of a cross on some church steps and prayed out loud for help. He was delivered from his temptation.

8. Matt paid all his bar bills, continued to look for the fiddler whose fiddle he had helped to steal, and gave his extra money to charity.

9. Matt would tip his hat in reverence to the Holy Name.

10. Accept any reasonable answer, including: Matt slept on boards, with a block of wood for a pillow, holding a statue of Mary and Jesus. He only slept for three and a half hours per night, waking up early to pray.

11. A person wishing to follow True Devotion entrusts, or consecrates, himself/herself to Jesus in Mary. He/She entrusts all his/her prayers, actions, and virtuous works to the hands of Mary. The soul trusts Mary to form in him/her the image of Jesus.

12. "When I get hold of a book like that, I always pray to Our Blessed Lady; and I believe that she always inspires me to take the correct meaning out of the words."

13. "Whenever I wanted a particular favor from heaven, I asked Matt to pray for it. His prayers were never refused."

14. Sean T. O'Ceallaigh was his name. He became the President of Ireland.

15. Matt Talbot died on June 7, 1925, on Trinity Sunday.

16. Everyone was astonished that Matt wore chains as a penance.

St. Josephine Bakhita

1. Sr. Bakhita forgave them and prayed for them.

2. Accept any reasonable answer, including: Bakhita was not mistreated in any way. She was cared for, dressed well, and her work was not hard. Bakhita was loved. She enjoyed peace and tranquility.

3. She had a strong feeling that she should follow her master there.

4. Bakhita would have been kidnapped again by pirates.

5. Bakhita was nursemaid for Mimmina, daughter of the Michielis.

6. Filled with a strange feeling, she asked the Man on the Cross, "Who are you? Why have they put you on the Cross?"

7. Bakhita wanted to nourish and practice her Faith, and she would have little opportunity for this living with the Michielis in Sudan.

8. Bakhita received Baptism, Confirmation, and Holy Communion.

9. Bakhita heard a call to consecrate her life to God.

10. She met with the Cardinal of Venice, Giuseppe Sarto, who later became Pope St. Pius X.

11. Sr. Bakhita was so compassionate because she had suffered much herself.

12. "How many thousands of Africans would accept the faith, if only there were missionaries to tell them that God loves them and that Jesus Christ died for them?"

13. Sr. Bakhita loved Our Lady very much, and Saturday is the day of the week dedicated to her.

14. St. Bakhita was canonized on October 1st, during the Jubilee Year of 2000, the Year of Reconciliation.

Pope St. Pius X

1. All he wanted to be was a simple country priest.

2. Cardinal Sarto traveled to Rome to elect a new pope because Pope Leo XIII had died.

3. "I am unworthy. I am not qualified. Forget me!"

4. He prayed before a crucifix.

5. Giuseppe was an excellent student, and he received a scholarship.

6. Don Sarto established a night school and taught the adults himself. The payment he wanted was for his students to stop swearing.

7. ". . . a want of the knowledge of God and His truth."

8. Accept any reasonable answer, including: He gave away any spare money he had to the poor. He gave away any preaching stipend he received. He tutored poor boys who had vocations to the priesthood. He gave away household food to the poor.

9. Accept any reasonable answer, including: He gave them a regular course on meditation and instruction. He helped poor seminarians. He took care of sick seminarians. He bought warm cloaks for them.

10. The local government had been hostile to the Church. Or: The government tried to drive the Church out of existence.

11. He asked that the people assemble in church to attend Mass with him.

12. The Congress was held in reparation for the many sacrileges committed against Jesus in the Blessed Sacrament.

13. Accept any reasonable answer, including: He emancipated the Church from slavery. His actions inspired a whole generation of dedicated young men to join the priesthood, and these men renewed the Faith in France. There was no more political interference in the appointment of bishops.

14. He lowered the age at which children could receive First Communion to age seven, he urged the faithful to receive Holy Communion daily if possible, and he made it easier for sick people to receive.

15. He wrote the document *Pascendi*, in which he outlined the errors of Modernism and suggested remedies; and he mandated that all priests take the "Oath Against Modernism."

16. "God will provide."

17. . . . had healed people.

18. Many thought that the Pope died of a broken heart.